DECADE OF THE
WOLF

Previous books by Douglas W. Smith

The Wolves of Yellowstone, co-authored with Mike Phillips

Previous books by Gary Ferguson

The Great Divide: The Rocky Mountains in the American Mind
Hawks Rest: A Season in the Remote Heart of Yellowstone
Shouting at the Sky: Troubled Teens and the Promise of the Wild

www.wildwords.net

DOUGLAS W. SMITH & GARY FERGUSON

DECADE OF THE
WOLF

RETURNING THE WILD TO
YELLOWSTONE

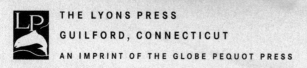

THE LYONS PRESS
GUILFORD, CONNECTICUT
AN IMPRINT OF THE GLOBE PEQUOT PRESS

Photographs courtesy of:

Chapter openers: Pages 3, 77, 85: Bob Landis; pp 19, 35, 59, 93, 97, 133:
National Park Service/Jim Peaco; pp 45, 63, 109, 137: National Park Service/Douglas
Smith; p 117: Bill Campbell; p 169: Mark Miller.

Insert: Pages 1–3, 28–29: Mark Miller; pp 4 (top), 5 (bottom): National Park
Service/Jim Peaco; p 4 (bottom): Jeanne Ross; pp 6–7, 18–19, 21 (top), 22–23, 25
(top): Doug Dance; p 8: Bill Campbell; pp 9 (top), 20 (top), 20 and 21 (bottom),
25 (bottom), 26 and 27 (bottom): Bob Landis; pp 9 (bottom), 24: National Park
Service/Dan Stahler; pp 10–11, 14–17, 26 (bottom), 27, 30–31: National Park
Service/Douglas Smith; pp 12–13: Dale and Elva Paulson; p 26 (top) Monty Sloan;
p 32 (Clockwise from top): National Park Service; Turner Endangered Species
Fund; Bill Campbell; National Park Service/Debra Guernsey; National Park
Service/Douglas Smith; National Park Service, National Park Service; National Park
Service/Douglas Smith; National Park Service/Douglas Smith (center).

The Lyons Press is an imprint of The Globe Pequot Press

10 9 8 7 6 5 4 3 2 1

Printed in the United States of America

Book design and composition by Diane Gleba Hall

ISBN 1-59228-700-X

Library of Congress Cataloging-in-Publication Data is available on file.

for Christine

CONTENTS

Contents

ACKNOWLEDGMENTS

To mention all of the people involved in the first ten years of the Yellowstone wolf reintroduction would by itself fill a small book. Our thanks and admiration go out to them all. In writing *Decade of the Wolf*, we're especially indebted to those who lent critical comments to the manuscript, including Ed Bangs, Rick McIntyre, Rolf Peterson, Jane Ferguson, Judy McHale, our agent Joe Regal, and of course our editor at The Lyons Press, Ann Treistman. John Varley and Dave Mech were also enormously helpful. Debra Guernsey and Daniel Stahler of the Wolf Project offered not only valuable insights, but helped with fact checking and data compilation. We greatly appreciate each of several outstanding photographers, including Bob Landis, Doug Dance, Mark Miller, Bill Campbell, Monty Sloan, and Dale and Elva Paulson, whose careful eye and generous spirit have become such an important part of this work. (Thanks too to many fine amateurs who shared images with us—we regret having simply run out of room!) Finally, co-author Doug Smith's wife Christine deserves heartfelt gratitude for many reasons, not the least of which is the sacrifice of family time she made for the sake of this project. Here's hoping, Christine, that our lives can now return to normal.

Special Note

The stories in this book are based on the field experiences of biologist Douglas W. Smith, combined with insights from nature writer Gary Ferguson. They represent neither the official views of Yellowstone National Park nor the National Park Service. Dr. Smith, who currently serves as head of the Yellowstone Wolf Recovery Project, co-authored this book entirely on his own time, and has received no financial compensation.

DECADE OF THE
WOLF

CHAPTER 1
A PASSION FOR
WOLVES

August 3, 2004. It's been a hectic summer. Phone calls and faxes and e-mails, all of it coming in doses big enough to have kept me hobbled to the desk instead of out in the field. More than a month has passed since I squeezed into the backseat of the yellow Piper Super Cub parked down at Gardiner Airport, snapped the seat belt together, slipped on the headphones and went airborne, purring across the high country on a search for the

fifteen wolf packs now making their homes in Yellowstone. If there's any shred of consolation it's only that up until recently the summer flying has been less than gratifying, what with the northern Rockies having been ravaged by six years of drought. Long ago the green swales of Yellowstone bled to brown, exposing dirt where once there were wildflowers and grasses; fires have roared across the backcountry—ten thousand, twenty thousand acres at a time. On more than one occasion I've peered down from the airplane and swore I could see the animals suffering.

As of late, though, there's come to much of the park fine measures of rain. Grasses are tall and thick, flowers everywhere. And rising in me is a yearning to savor it all, this easy month of August. For these few weeks animals are free of the edginess that tends to grip them at other times of year. Wolves are relaxed, even oblivious, plopped down in the shade of their summer rendezvous sites. I'm wanting to slow down, too—take it all in, pay attention not just to wolves but to the nature that surrounds them. Match my pace with the pace of the season.

I meet pilot Roger Stradley at the usual time for summer flights, 6:30 in the morning. We start early because of the nearly constant promise of afternoon wind and thunderstorms—tough on pilots and passengers alike. Rising through the clear morning light we find the area around Gardiner still looking parched, desiccated. Yet by the time we're past the foothills of the national park, crossing lands sitting at roughly 6,500 feet, the vegetation begins to perk up in a big way; by 7,000-foot Swan Lake Flats the place looks downright lush. It's like flying into paradise.

Finding Yellowstone's wolves is a matter of following signals given off by radio collars worn by certain animals from each pack. First up on the checklist are the Swan Lake wolves, just south of Mammoth. In no time at all we find the bulk of the group—six animals bedded down together and maybe a lone pup among them, though it's hard to say, since by now the young have grown so big it's tough to distinguish them from the adults. Continuing to check radio signals one-by-one we soon discover

*someone on our list is missing, only to locate him a few minutes later
with two other wolves near a freshly killed bull elk. Not in possession of
the carcass, though. Not even close. That privilege belongs to three grizzly bears, shaking their massive heads and slicing at the hide with their
powerful paws. Though nowhere near as quick as the wolf the bear is far
stronger. Long ago he figured he could hijack pretty much any wolf kill
he wanted, reducing those who took the prize in the first place to little
more than hungry bystanders.*

*On we fly, tracking our way to the Geode Creek Pack (unable to find
wolf Number 392), then Rose Creek and Agate Creek (four black pups),
on to Slough Creek (six pups along with 378 are missing), to Druid Peak
(gone from the Lamar Valley, totally bumming out the wolf watchers),
to Specimen Ridge (all huddled at 9,000 feet, so tightly bunched together we have a hard time counting the five pups). After all that it's
time for Mollie's Pack. Living as they do in the Pelican Valley, far from
the chaos of cars and tourists, free even of the bother of other wolf
packs, home ground for Mollie's Pack is serene. Far below us Pelican
Creek does a quiet rumba through long runs of meadow grass, past hot
springs, in no hurry at all to make its final plunge into the cold, blue
waters of Yellowstone Lake. The first of the Mollie wolves we locate,
Number 379, is by all appearances tuned in to much the same music,
sacked out in the shade of a small cluster of fir and spruce, indifferent
to the drone of our plane circling overhead.*

*Across the past decade my work as a wolf biologist has changed in
subtle yet significant ways. During the first three years of the project
we knew every single wolf intimately. Back then I'd fly over this landscape just as I'm doing today, but more often than not be consumed by
specifics: whether or not wolf Number 9 could hang in there for another year, maybe have another litter of pups; or if Number 39, whose
mate was shot by a poacher, would be able to hook up with another
partner. If only we could get through another year, I often thought, get*

just one more batch of pups, then the population would be on its feet. Today it's a different world. We know fairly well the fifty-five animals now collared—ten or fifteen of these we know really well—but there are plenty of others we don't. Whereas once we thought only of the struggles of individuals and their packs to become anchored in this new home, now our thoughts rest in matters of population dynamics, of the links between predator and prey. The relationships that drive our work, in other words, are these days less anchored in the intimate than the ecological.

Still, even now it's hard to overstate the impact of working with this animal. I recall several years ago flying fairly low in the spotter plane, when we crossed directly over a wolf. As it looked up I could see its eyes, and they were magnificent, bright and burning. While a lot of animals in that sort of circumstance would be nearly overcome with fear, here was one tossing out a stare that seemed brimming with confidence. The wolf looked hard at us, following us with its gaze for a couple of seconds. Then it merely stepped away, back into its element. The encounter was so vivid that the pilot, like me, seemed barely able to contain himself. "Whoo-hoo!" he shouted. "That was big stuff!" Admittedly, such meetings don't happen often—I've been flying wolves for twenty-five years, and have seen such things maybe only half a dozen times. But it's something that sticks with you long afterward.

We work the nearby forest for a while, sure that hiding under the branches are four or five Mollie's pups, then slide over to find the aged alpha male, Number 193, in a snooze fest of his own some four hundred yards away. His aging mate, the alpha female, is out in the valley, bedded down but clearly alert. Next comes Number 378, splayed in grass so deep it takes two circles in the plane to finally figure out that there really is a wolf in there. Given he's from a pack living well to the north— or at least was collared with them—finding him here at all is a bit of a surprise. But Mollie's Pack was this wolf's original family, the group he

6

was born to back in 2001. He probably still feels a certain kinship with them—ties that even now, three years later, keep calling.

Not far from the alpha female young wolf Number 343 starts "wanging in"—a term we use for strong radio signals, telling us an animal is very close. Before actually seeing him, though, we glimpse something else: six grizzlies, including two big boys pushing 500 pounds, as well as a sow with a cub-of-the-year—the entire crew gathered around a dead bull elk. For his part Wolf 343 has wisely decided to remain above the fray, bedding down nearby on a small cut in a grass-covered bank. What's unusual about this sighting is the presence of a sow grizzly with cub. Female bears with young typically avoid such get-togethers, given that both wolves as well as male bears have a reputation for killing their young. Even now the little one is clearly agitated, standing on his hind legs and looking in on the carcass, but not daring to go any closer. On our next pass I notice still another bruin bedded down not ten yards from 343, waiting his own turn at the table, each unconcerned about the other. In fact from my vantage point both bear and wolf appear to be wearing that wistful, faraway look that comes easily on the heels of summer in Yellowstone.

♦ ♦ ♦

THEY WERE once among the most abundant predators in all of North America—at least five subspecies of wolves,[1] perhaps two million animals,[2] spread across the continent from coast to coast. Hunting whitetails in the lowland forests of the East, where now stand the skyscrapers of Boston and New York; howling in the dark of long, unbroken runs of chestnut and hickory in the central Midwest. Running the shores of the Great Lakes, slipping through the big trees of the Pacific Northwest, hunting in the cool of night in the arid deserts of Arizona and New Mexico. But despite their numbers, despite their speed and strength and remarkable cleverness, it took just a couple centuries for us to wipe them from well over 95 percent of their former range in the conterminous

United States.[3] By the time I came into the world there were a mere
five hundred left, mostly cornered in the remote regions of the upper
Midwest.[4] In part, of course, the extermination can be said to be a triumph of man's astonishing ability to kill that which either frightens or
inconveniences him. But in a very real sense it's also a reflection of the
fact that, unlike coyotes and mountain lions and even black bear, all
of which have found ways to more or less coexist with people, wolves
have shown no such inclination. Instead they're prone always to stand
their ground, not bending for the sake of living amicably alongside
humans.

Which makes it all the more striking to think that in the ten years
since wolves came home to Yellowstone, they've become for thousands
of people a symbol of a wilderness ideal, a fascination kindled amidst
growing threats to America's last untrammeled places. Today less than
5 percent of the nation is protected wilderness. Of these places not even
a handful are big enough to support healthy populations of large carnivores. Wildlife winter range in the Rockies is being lost to development
at a staggering pace; in parts of Colorado alone land is being subdivided
at the rate of ten acres every hour. Despite the dramatic success of the
Yellowstone wolf reintroduction, no one can say for sure how these animals will fare in the long run. Their fates, after all, like the fates of most
creatures, are connected to strands in the web of life over which they
have no control.

Jim Hammill, who presided over the natural recovery of wolves in
the upper peninsula of Michigan, tells of being a small boy in 1960, out
chopping wood with his father in the North Woods. At one point during that chore he recalls his dad stopping and pointing toward a small
hill not far away. "That's where I saw the last wolf in this country," he
told Jim. "It's gone now. And nothing is the same."[5] When I first flew
over Yellowstone National Park in 1994 I had much the same feeling,
a strong sensation that for all the beauty of this landscape something

wasn't quite right. Like Jim Hammill's dad, I too had grown accustomed to the ambience of wolves—a sensation based not just on their intriguing behavior, but on the spirit they impart to their surroundings. Something akin to the attitude offered by famed wildlife biologists Olaus and Adolph Murie, who considered wolves the means by which to measure the basic integrity of wilderness. Or the notions of Aldo Leopold—the man who first recommended wolf reintroduction for Yellowstone back in 1944—as in his heartrending passage of regret at having shot one of the last wolves in New Mexico, witnessing in its eyes the dying of a "fierce green fire."[6]

That image of Aldo Leopold bringing a rifle to his shoulder, taking aim and pulling the trigger, only to find himself a moment later overcome by sadness at the dying of something truly wild, suggests much about America's relationship with wolves. Through this one animal we've expressed both our best and worst inclinations—in some moments moved to feats of great generosity, in others bound by thoughtless convention. And every now and then, going well beyond Leopold, engaging in baffling acts of cruelty.

Even today, at the very time thousands of people are coming from all over the world for a chance to glimpse the wild wolves of Yellowstone, individuals in northwest Wyoming are lacing hot dogs with powerful poisons like 1080 and Temik in an attempt to kill the animals, instead killing dozens of beloved pets. Since the first wolves walked free again in Yellowstone in 1995, at least thirty have been illegally killed in the immediate area. Websites have sprung up coaching viewers on how to destroy wolves. In central Idaho, also part of the 1995 reintroduction project, one biologist gave a dire description of a recent flurry of criminal poaching there: "Hunting season has arrived, and the wolves in Idaho are dropping like flies." Much as in the Middle Ages, when the wolf was touted by church leaders as proof of Satan walking the earth, in this day and age there are some who would infuse it with yet another kind of symbolic power, one having to do with a fierce hatred for the land management policies of the federal government.

When I first started working with this predator I considered it mostly from a biological perspective, as a scientist on the trail of a rich and fascinating piece of the natural world. Recently, though, that outlook is often overwhelmed by a struggle to endure a furious, even brutal polarization between those who despise wolves, and those who think they can do no wrong. Caught in the middle, and in ways strangely ignored by both sides, is the animal itself. A creature concerned only with the difficult, risky job of being a wolf. People are often surprised to learn that the average age of wolves in Yellowstone at time of death—at least those we collar, and so are able to follow throughout their lives—is only 3.4 years. Despite their cleverness and their high level of social functioning, despite astonishing determination, their lives unfold against great risk—from having their skulls kicked in and limbs and teeth broken, to death at the hands of rival packs. They don't outsmart their environment. But they do roll well with the punches.

As far as we can tell, with the return of the gray wolf the region called greater Yellowstone has reclaimed its full complement of historic mammals; indeed, the area is now commonly described as the largest generally intact ecosystem in the temperate world. This project says a lot about the value Americans place on the creatures of the wild, even those that can be troublesome on occasion. For that matter the entire restoration was guided by directives contained in the Endangered Species Act—a law created to ground a decades-old cornerstone of science that says the healthiest, most stable natural systems tend to be those with high levels of biodiversity. It was specifically the flowering of that knowledge that led the National Park Service—the same agency that killed the last wolf in Yellowstone in 1926—to commit seventy years later to an extraordinary effort to bring them back. Admittedly, some consider the act of returning the very animal we spent millions of dollars eradicating as a sign of madness. But to others, including many scientists, this has been a move filled with hope—a clear indication that we've finally started to move beyond a longstanding body of myth that treated all predators as if they were God's great mistake. To those who value ecological health, the wolf has become a powerful touchstone to the wisdom of managing the last pieces of wild America with a generous commitment to wholeness. Of course we'll never realize Thoreau's fondest wish, "to know an entire heaven and an entire earth"; the needs of humans will likely always triumph over the needs of other species. Yet to the extent the wolf is forcing us to pay attention to its myriad links and connections—more significant than any of us could imagine—it will help us more fully embrace the true wonders of the wild.

It's worth mentioning that perhaps more than any other place in America, the nature-based dramas unfolding in Yellowstone play to eager audiences around the world. Even in the earliest stages of this work, when we were still in Canada, catching wolves for later release in the national park, it took little time before our activities were headline news from China to Europe, Australia to South America. Many people in these other cultures have been watching for reasons that go well beyond the thrill of the wolf itself. Some questioned whether a wealthy nation like ours, one increasingly prone to sharing its concerns about the loss of species diversity in third world countries, was willing to make the sacrifices necessary to effect a major restoration in its own backyard. Some biologists consider bringing wolves home to Yellowstone, northwest Montana, and central Idaho to be among the biggest conservation projects of the twentieth century—a twenty-year effort directed not on a regional level, but by the full Congress of the United States. Such a commitment, matched by what is a truly remarkable success, will unquestionably have impacts on conservation efforts around the globe.

✦ ✦ ✦

In truth it's hard for me to even recall a life without wolves. For over a quarter century I've been working with them as a biologist—in the piney woods of Minnesota, along the rocky shores of Isle Royale National Park, and for the past decade, in the great sweeps of sage and lodgepole and grass-covered vales of Yellowstone. But long before any of that, while still just a boy, I spent a good half-dozen years simply day-dreaming about them—staring north from my home in the maple and beech woodlands of the Midwest, conjuring images of wild country un-folding across the Canadian border and running all the way to the Arctic. A land of snow and birch and pine, of rivers and lakes. A land of wolves.

Happily, it was my great fortune to have been raised with my feet in the dirt, the seasons of childhood unfolding in the midst of a summer camp and school of horsemanship my parents owned in rural north-eastern Ohio. There were hay rides in fall, a maple syrup operation in winter and early spring, and throughout the school year, week-long na-ture studies designed by my father for area school groups. For reasons that even today I don't entirely understand it was there, roaming the woods either alone or with my dog, that the idea of wolves first began taking hold, soon to become a driving force in my life. By my senior year in high school I'd secured a volunteer position with Purdue University's Erich Klinghammer, who was conducting behavioral studies with a captive colony of wolves in Indiana. Part of this research involved people actu-ally bonding with wolves, a feat that can only be accomplished by start-ing when pups are no more than a couple weeks old. And so it was that my first lucky break in the world of wolf research was to serve as a "mother" to four little ones named Sirgei, Sasha, Mephisto, and Faust. Hour after hour I stayed with them, literally around the clock—nursing and feeding, cleaning up, even sleeping with them. Due to the constraints of my senior project I ended up having to leave just before reaching that critical point when wolves finally manage to forge bonds with humans. Even so, years later I visited Klinghammer at his Wolf Park facility in northern Indiana, where I got the chance to go into the pen with one of my former charges, Sirgei—by now a large adult. He jumped up on me, a paw on each shoulder, looking me in the face, studying me intently, as if he might have some vague recollection of who I was.

From there would come more wolf work, over ten years' worth, much of it with famed wolf biologist Rolf Peterson on Isle Royale. Later, as part of my masters and PhD degrees—both of which focused on beavers—I was lucky enough to walk thousands of miles alone through the North Woods, checking trap lines, live capturing some two thousand beavers across four national parks, including Voyageurs and Grand Portage in Minnesota, Apostle Islands in Wisconsin, and Isle Royale in Michigan. And while the work wasn't focused on wolves it was nonetheless in the thick of wolf country. What's more, I always managed to get wolf jobs on the side with either Rolf or Dave Mech, making this one of the most satisfying times of my life.

In 1994, having at last finished my fieldwork for my PhD, I learned of a job working with wolves in Yellowstone. This was to be a reintroduction, bringing animals into an ecosystem that hadn't seen a viable breeding population for some seventy years. I remember clearly the day the program's project leader, Mike Phillips—a man who'd been one of my hiking partners at Isle Royale thirteen years earlier—called to offer me the job. It was a phone call that left me both thrilled and troubled. I was by then, after all, firmly attached to the North Woods, had in fact a short time earlier been given the promise of a job working as a wildlife biologist in beautiful Voyageurs National Park. I talked it out with Rolf Peterson, who in that pleasantly understated fashion of many Scandinavians told me that

Voyageurs would be "a solid second choice." The Yellowstone project, he seemed to be saying, was the opportunity of a lifetime.

Over the past decade I've become deeply connected to the northern Rocky Mountains—and specifically to this, the world's first national park—whereas of this writing some 170 wolves are running free. This from a starting point of thirty-one wolves brought down from Canada across two years—fourteen animals in three groups in the spring of 1995, then seventeen more in four separate groups the following year, in 1996. From a biological standpoint alone this effort has been hugely significant. Of all the places in North America where wolves still roam less than a dozen are sanctuaries: Isle Royale, Denali, Voyageurs, and Glacier national parks in the United States; Wood Buffalo, Banff, Jasper, Kluane, Riding Mountain national parks, as well as Algonquin Provincial Park in Canada.

Along with these locations are lands not designated as preserves but which still offer security for wolves—portions of Alaska, Yukon and Northwest Territories, Nunavut, and the coast of British Columbia—yet these areas may not be able to offer protection beyond the next fifty to one hundred years. Farther to the south is Isle Royale, which while as an island offers great safety, is so small that its wolf population may in the long run not be sustainable. Elsewhere in the Lower 48 parks and preserves have leaky boundaries, where wolves routinely cross out and are killed. (Happily, Algonquin Provincial Park recently shored up some of those leaks, extending a buffer out from the park border, which offers wolves an extra measure of protection.) To this dwindling list we can now add Yellowstone. It's hardly perfect, being both modest in size and riddled with dangers along its borders. Nonetheless, bringing gray wolves back to this most southern preserve is a spectacular accomplishment.

To return the animal that was for thousands of years top predator of the Yellowstone landscape is to change nearly everything about the place. In a very real sense, with the return of wolves we've gained the opportunity to glimpse the dynamic forces of nature that drove this region before the coming of the Europeans. Many of the park's elk herds, for example—the primary prey species for these wolves—now face an additional risk of predation. As a result, in some places these elk have changed their behavior—moving away from certain feeding areas along park streams and rivers that have poor visibility. Preliminary research suggests that such movements are allowing willow, cottonwood shoots, and other vegetation to be "released," flourishing where they haven't for decades. With the return of such plants have come beaver, and with the construction of beaver dams, a loose toss of back channels and still ponds perfect for muskrat, amphibians, fish, waterfowl, even songbirds like yellow and Wilson's warblers. Likewise as coyote populations have dwindled in the face of wolves, some of this smaller canine's favorite prey, including antelope fawns and red fox, may enjoy higher survival rates. And on it goes. As astonishing as it may sound, in the decades to come wolves may prove no less fundamental to the life of Yellowstone than water is to the Everglades. "Ecologically speaking," says John Varley, the extraordinarily capable director of the Yellowstone Center for Resources, "wolf reintroduction is hands down the most exciting thing to happen in the history of the national park."

For those of us working as scientists, with every roll of the seasons come new questions, new opportunities for learning. And always, a constant reminder that just when we think we have wolves figured out, they're bound to prove us wrong. The combination of a habitat previously unpopulated by wolves, along with this animal's astonishing ability to adapt, have created for biologists something akin to astronauts landing on an untouched planet. This reintroduction has brought with it the prospect of learning how wolves settle landscapes, kill prey, deal with interpack skirmishes, socialize, mate, raise their pups, even fend off grizzly bears. And while it's true that many of such behaviors have been looked at before, never have we had the visibility afforded by Yellowstone. Some researchers claim that what they learn in a given year in this national park, would in other places take a decade.[7]

Relatively little research had been done, for instance, in documenting the life histories of individual animals. How long do they live? How many pups does a wolf have in her lifetime? How many of those pups live past one year, or for that matter, go on to breed themselves? At what age do wolves stop breeding? At what age do they stop killing prey, if ever? Though some of these questions had been addressed anecdotally, few had been examined over time, in quantitative fashion. Because we were able to document the beginning of this population—as well as thanks to how visibly accessible the Yellowstone wolves proved to be— we were uniquely poised to unravel some of these more subtle aspects of their natural history. As one example, to date we've documented the lifetime reproductive success of twenty-six different females, and that number's growing.

Some frustrated with the wolf have suggested that, given the increasing demand on western landscapes, we should manage Yellowstone more as a game farm, an outdoor zoo, fencing in or otherwise controlling those species that get into trouble now and then outside the park.[8] But in a very real sense such a move would hobble us, as well. As even Sigmund Freud pointed out—and clearly, Sigmund was no nature boy—wild preserves and the creatures that occupy them can be just as important to a culture's mental health as fantasy is to an individual; remove either one, he seemed to say, and neurosis will follow. By piquing our imaginations, by sparking in us a sense of wonder, Yellowstone's wolves have done much to invigorate our sense of place, even our sense of generosity, rekindling relationships that allow us to again feel at home in the world.

◆ ◆ ◆

Having finished the work of checking on Mollie's Pack, pilot Roger Stradley turns the yellow Piper down the east side of Yellowstone Lake— one of my favorite stretches of this wild, meandering commute. As usual, today's radio tracking has been fast and furious, requiring plenty of focus—punching in this frequency, deleting that one, hearing something from two prior frequencies and moving the antennae left and right— watching to see where Roger's going to bank the plane. Here along Yellowstone Lake, though, with some twenty miles to go before reaching the Delta Pack, I can take a breath. Gaze out the window into the blue water below, watch Columbine, Beaverdam, Trapper, and Mountain creeks push down their rocky beds.

The Yellowstone River Delta, namesake for the Delta Pack, is by any measure among the most beautiful places in the entire park. Sometimes I travel here after human activity winds down in the fall, thrilling at how the place seems to drip with wildness; now and then I'll pull back the reins on my horse, Amos, stopping for no other reason than to feel the silence. True, it's grizzly country—so much so that some of the park staff who've visited here swear they'll never come again. But that just makes me like it more. As it turns out, on this day the Delta Pack is nowhere to be found—not by their den, not by their rendezvous site. In the end we find only one wolf from the entire pack, then feel the wind coming up, prompting Roger to turn the Super Cub toward home. On the way back to Gardiner, near the park's northern boundary, we pick up the Nez Perce, Biscuit Basin, Cougar Creek, and Gibbon Meadows packs, locating them in what's fast becoming blustery weather.

By the time our wheels touch down again we've logged four-and-a-half hours. And while my knees and butt are well aware of it, my mind and spirit feel renewed—even with a dozen phone calls, fifty e-mails, and several unscheduled appointments and meetings no doubt waiting for me back at the office. Through all that chatter I'll be drawing on memories of having just seen eleven grizzlies, two black bears, fifty-five wolves, a hundred elk, two moose, several hundred bison, and five deer—all against a backdrop of a green and verdant Yellowstone. Leaving the airport I'm already thinking maybe I should saddle Amos this fall and take another one of those rides down the Delta. I know that horse, and I'm telling you, he'd really like that.

CHAPTER 2
THE
CROSSING

Even to Carter Niemeyer—a barge of a man, able to

churn upstream in the roughest waters—it seemed a bleak

beginning. He'd rolled north out of Montana in 1994 in a fit of

late-autumn wind and snow, bound for the wilds of Alberta, sent as

clean-up man for a wolf capture effort still half-formed and full of dis-

array. A lawsuit against the wolf reintroduction was working its way

through the courts, leaving many of us wondering if the project would happen at all. Meanwhile wire cable had arrived in Canada from the States, intended for Canadian trappers to use in making the modified snares needed to capture wolves ultimately bound for Yellowstone. Unfortunately it was the wrong gauge, coyote wire, too thin to even begin to hold an animal as powerful as a wolf. No holding facilities were in place. There were no local vets lined up to work the project.

In addition, promises had been made several months earlier to various Canadian wolf trappers, offering goodly sums of money for the delivery of live animals to American biologists—roughly three times what they normally earned for pelts. But since those initial offers there'd been not another word, a slip-up in follow-through that put these highly independent men—guys already suspicious of anyone dimwitted enough to actually want live wolves—in the foulest of tempers. Now on the receiving end of their sour moods is the Yank sitting in their midst—the big one, Carter Niemeyer—who on this snowy afternoon finds himself twenty miles north of the village of Hinton, Alberta, in the living room of trapper Wade Berry, surrounded by a gaggle of beer-soaked woodsmen, the whole bunch hurling curses strong enough to make a longshoreman blush.

Failing to hear from the Americans the trappers have gone back to what they've done all along, which is kill wolves for pelts. Early on Wade takes Carter out to the fur shed to show him seven wolf hides on stretching boards. "This is what we do to wolves," he says. Carter shakes his head, tells him it doesn't make sense to kill for four or five hundred bucks, when he's offering close to fifteen hundred for the animals alive. Wade's not convinced. By late afternoon Carter is still swimming in insults, being told time and again to pack his bags and get his ass back home. "A real pissing match," Carter would later describe it. Sometime after the beer but before the homemade chokecherry wine gets poured, a trapper named Brad who works for Wade stomps in from the cold to announce he's got two dead wolves outside. Wade's a bit bleary, though still fuming, and he looks at Carter with a sneer.

"You ever skinned anything?"

"Yeah," Carter tells him. "I've skinned plenty." Which is sort of an understatement. Through his work both as an Animal Damage Control officer as well as a taxidermist Niemeyer has by this point probably slipped the pelts from some six thousand coyotes, not to mention bears, lions, even the occasional wolf. Unconvinced, Wade tells Brad to bring in the two dead wolves, right there into the living room. "I'm thinking maybe we should have a skinning contest," he says. "Ya know, Brad's our best skinner."

For a moment both would-be contestants seem confused. "You mean right here—in your house?" Carter says, scarcely able to believe what he's hearing, casting a doubtful look at Wade's wife, Karri. "Jeez, we'll get blood over everything."

"Hell with that," Wade scoffs. "We can replace the carpets."

And so it is that Carter Niemeyer, sent up north to kindle the collaring operation that will eventually land wolves in Yellowstone National Park, finds himself in the corner of a man's living room in northern Canada next to a burly, bearded trapper, knives and sharpening stones at the ready, each with a hundred and twenty pound wolf in his lap and blood everywhere, covering their hands, soaking through shirts and pants and long johns.

"I don't think we were really racing," Carter will explain later. "But I did get mine done first."

It's the spectacle that changes everything. The next thing Carter knows Wade's put aside insults in favor of some honest-to-goodness male bonding. He insists Carter have another round of chokecherry wine, then later, that he not drive back to Hinton but instead spend the night on the couch. "Wade had this little heeler-type dog that spent nights upstairs in the loft with him and Karri," recalls Carter. "Guess he wasn't feeling too good, 'cause every hour or so I'd hear the 'tap-tap-tap' of his toenails as he trotted down the steps of the ladder, crossed the living room to the kitchen where he puked all over the floor. Then came the tapping of toenails going back up the ladder again. Round after round of it, all night long."

The next morning Wade asks Carter if he still wants wolves. That confirmed, Wade tells him to head back to the Terra Vista Hotel in Hinton to get his stuff—collars, tools, sedatives, a jab stick, and an hour or so later he's in a pickup with Brad and Wade, driving up the highway in a blanket of blowing snow, heading for a trap line at the edge of Rock Lake. Once at the site Brad and Wade head off into the woods by themselves, and sure enough, before long find a wolf in a neck snare, alive but seriously hypothermic. They yell Carter over, and he wastes no time sedating the animal. Then, to Wade's total dismay, he hefts the wolf on his shoulders, carries it to the truck where he sticks it in the backseat, starts the engine and turns the heater on full blast. Soon after comes a shout—still another wolf—this one too caught with a snare around its neck, the animal cowering on the steep side of a stream bank in a small alcove. The place proves so hard to reach that in the end Wade and Brad have to hold Niemeyer upside down by his legs in order for him to reach the animal and tranquilize it. This one too goes into the backseat of the truck to be warmed. By now Wade is seriously tense, shooting nervous looks at Carter, wanting to make absolutely sure his new buddy has a good handle on just how long a shot of tranquilizer really lasts.

And just like that, Carter Niemeyer is neck-deep in wolves. In the closing weeks of 1994 other animals will be caught—most of them, thankfully, in modified snares—then transported by the same sort of pickup truck express to a newly located holding facility. Among them will be Number 7, an outstanding yearling female who in 1996 would go on to hook up with a male from another pack, thus creating the first naturally occurring wolf pack in Yellowstone. Reinforcements arrive from the States, including Steve Fritts, Val Asher, Alice Whitelaw, Jim Till, Joe Fontaine, and veterinarian Mark Johnson.

Order rises from chaos. Once captured in snares the wolves are collared and processed, then released again near the places where they were first taken, each returning quickly to its own pack. Later on those same individuals are located still again—this time by men in spotter planes tracking them by the signals being given off by their radio collars. On finding the wolves this time, though, helicopters are launched—as it turns out, in bitterly cold conditions, the thermometer stuck at roughly thirty degrees below zero. Biologists hang out the open doors of the aircraft with darting guns in hand, each man wrapped in thick layers of warm clothing, any exposed skin freezing in an instant. Their mission is to not only fire darts containing tranquilizer into the animals that were captured earlier, but also into as many of their pack mates as possible, no matter the age or gender. Some groups are darted out in open meadows, still others on frozen lake ice.

Back in the States, three acclimation pens have been constructed in the northern region of the national park—each about an acre in size, each meant to hold one family group. This idea of taking as many members as possible from three separate packs, as opposed to simply grabbing random wolves that may not know one another, plays on the strong bonds that exist between animals of the same group. The hope is that keeping families together will lower stress levels—important not just in the weeks of confinement to come, but also after the wolves walk free, when some might be tempted to make a mad dash back to Canada. Again, in this first year of capture the three groups—one for each acclimation pen—will contain a total of fourteen animals. The following winter, in 1996—the second and last time Canadian wolves are captured—will see four family groups from British Columbia, totaling seventeen more. The fate of wolves in Yellowstone will rest on the shoulders of these thirty-one animals.

To reach this point had taken more than twenty-five years. While the value of returning wolves to the world's first national park was seen by a handful of biologist as early as the 1940s, it wasn't until much later that there was strong political will to save the country's dwindling wildlife resources. Inspired in part by plummeting populations of whooping cranes, in 1966 Congress passed the Endangered Species Preservation Act. It allowed the Secretary of the Interior to make a list of endangered domestic native fish and wildlife, and also provided for expenditures of up to $15 million a year to purchase habitat for their protection. (The first outlay of such funds, by the way, was in 1968, used to purchase 2,300 acres in Florida for the National Key deer.)

This basic law was made stronger still in 1969, with the passage of the Endangered Species Conservation Act. Prompted in part by concerns over dwindling whale populations, the act prohibited the importation of threatened species—or any product made from them—no matter where in the world they happened to reside. Curiously, among the early challenges to this law was one coming from the Pentagon, who argued that sperm-whale oil was essential to submarine guidance systems. (Others would argue its importance in other industrial applications, including automatic transmission fluid.) Over time the 1969 act was found to lack the necessary "teeth" for effective enforcement. Before long, scientists and politicians alike were calling for still stronger measures of protection.

And so it was that 1973 saw the creation of the Endangered Species Act, passed by Congress with nearly unanimous support. It was a landmark piece of legislation. For starters, the ESA made a distinction between species actually endangered and those merely threatened. It also allowed for the protection of not just animals, but plants, too. Finally, it permitted the listing of species that were scarce or absent in only part of their range—a key factor in bringing the gray wolf back to Yellowstone. Once a species was placed on the list, the law required that a plan be crafted outlining specific steps for recovery. On signing the legislation on December 28th, 1973, President Richard Nixon echoed the sentiments of millions of Americans: "Nothing is more priceless and more worthy of preservation," he said, "than the rich array of animal life with which our country has been blessed."

◆ ◆ ◆

MAYBE IT'S FITTING that the capture of wolves bound for Yellowstone should begin with such big helpings of craziness. The years leading up to the reintroduction, after all, had been long on turmoil, short on common sense. Even the federal agency ultimately responsible for such projects, the U.S. Fish and Wildlife Service, was at times anything but enthused about the prospect of a reintroduction. In some years only Yellowstone National Park continued to quietly suggest that wolves had a place in a healthy ecosystem. "At one point," recalls Northern Rocky Mountain Wolf Coordinator Ed Bangs, "the director of the U.S. Fish and Wildlife Service told us that 'the only wolf coming into Montana is the one on my tie.' "

On the other hand, John Varley recalls attending a congressional committee hearing in 1991 where he watched dumbfounded as Republican senators from across the West lectured the committee on why they needed to go ahead with the project. "None of these people were wolf lovers. But Senator McClure, the chair of the Senate Interior Committee, had been arguing for years that an experimental reintroduction was far better than having wolves show up on their own. 'This way,' he said, 'we get to set the rules.' The rest of us just sat there, stunned." Likewise Varley remembers William Penn Mott, director of the National Park Service under Ronald Reagan, being a critical force for this reintroduction. "Both in front of congress and in front of the public, it was Mott who talked most often about the need for wolves in Yellowstone." Then again, Varley also recalls one of the longest afternoons of his life being when he gave the wolf pitch to the annual meeting of the Montana Stockgrowers. "They were hissing me. They were booing, throwing catcalls. It even upset the group's leaders—up there holding their arms out, trying to quiet the crowd."

As support grew for the idea of reintroduction, in 1992 the government started seeking public comments, holding meetings in scattered cities and towns throughout the intermountain West—gatherings that sometimes had all the appearance of troops massing for battle. Those people submitting comments from outside the region were heavily in favor of the project. (Four years later, in 1996, a national poll conducted by Colorado State University showed between 75 percent and 82 percent of the public, irrespective of their political affiliation, strongly supporting the reintroduction.) Here in the northern Rockies, though, the sides were more evenly divided, each showing no shortage of zeal. As conservationist Hank Fischer recalls in his book *Wolf Wars*, proponents and opponents alike descended en masse on capital cities like Helena, Montana, the latter holding signs declaring the wolf to be "The Saddam Hussein of the Animal World." Armed guards stood at the doors of the public meetings. One man testifying against the project seemed to sum up the feelings of the opposition well, declaring that "only a brain-dead son-of-a-bitch would favor reintroduction of wolves."

By the time the public comment period for the Environmental Impact Statement was over, some 160,000 remarks had arrived on the doorstep of the U.S. Fish and Wildlife Service—at the time, more than for any other similar document in American history. Again, the vast majority were in favor of the reintroduction. Yet as capture efforts got underway in Canada several lawsuits were launched—actions Judge William Downes ended up lumping together, his logic being that each one contested how the reintroduction was handled under provisions of the Endangered Species Act. That move made for some strange bedfellows, including a pairing of the Sierra Club Legal Defense Fund (not tied to the Sierra Club, and these days known as the Earth Justice Legal Defense Fund) with the American Farm Bureau.

The suit brought by the Sierra Club Legal Defense Fund insisted that the reintroduced wolves should be classified as endangered, rather than the "experimental, nonessential" population designated by the U.S. Fish and Wildlife Service. That designation, made by virtue of a special provision within the Endangered Species Act, was chosen to allow more management flexibility than would otherwise be permitted under the "endangered" listing. Under experimental, nonessential status, if a wolf ventured onto private property the landowner could chase it off—so long as he didn't injure it. More significantly, should a wolf attack livestock the rancher could legally kill it—a scenario that's actually played out over the past decade a good half-dozen times. The Sierra Club Legal Defense Fund team argued that any wolf already living in Montana—animals that immigrated on their own and therefore had full protection of the Endangered Species Act—would merely by crossing into the Idaho or Yellowstone "recovery zones" have their level of protection lowered. This was plain bad science, the litigants claimed—and even worse, bad management. Yet more than a dozen of the best North American wolf scientists thought otherwise, calling the experimental designation a reasonable tool for getting the job of reintroduction done without placing unnecessary burden on local residents.

For their part, the Farm Bureau claimed the reintroduction violated basic procedures of the Endangered Species Act—an interesting twist, given how often that organization has shown a fierce dislike for the ESA, having on several occasions sued to weaken it. The Farm Bureau suit led to a hold being placed on the project literally while wolves were en route to Yellowstone from Canada, confining the animals to their transport kennels. This was a heartbreaking situation. To finally get the wolves into the park, as per the approved plan, and then be told by the court that they were to remain in their tiny shipping kennels, unable even to be released into fenced acclimation pens, was by sheer virtue of its cruelty a hard pill to swallow. After waiting nervously well into the night we finally received word to release into the pens. Not wanting another minute's delay, four of us hiked to the sites in the wee hours and pulled open the doors on the kennels, allowing the wolves to at long last take their first steps on Yellowstone ground. Included in that group was biologist Wayne Brewster, a key national park administrator who had much to do with making this reintroduction happen in the first place. Heading back down the trail after releasing wolves into the Rose Creek Pen, around two o'clock in the morning, I recall him stopping, casting a reflective look. "Just think," he said. "This is something no one's ever done—or will ever do again."

This legal action by the Farm Bureau had another consequence, too. When the lawsuit was first filed the judge actually put a hold on our efforts in Canada—delaying capture operations for a time, forcing us to operate later in the winter than we'd originally planned. From the very beginning, this reintroduction was designed to avoid having wolves stuck in acclimation pens during the February breeding season, on the off chance that restraining them at this time in their yearly life cycle might prove too stressful. But these legal delays gave us no choice, forcing us to place wolves in pens smack in the middle of breeding season. To our surprise—and without question, our great relief—the pens ended up having little effect, with four of the seven groups breeding despite captivity. (It's interesting to consider that at our sister project in Idaho, where wolves were never held in acclimation pens, there was in the first year no discernable breeding activity.)

Ironically, the delay caused by the Farm Bureau suit inadvertently improved the success of the reintroduction. By late winter, the time when the wolves finally walked free, elk and other ungulates were at their weakest, vulnerable from having endured months of snow and cold. That made the wolves' job of taking prey much easier—a fact that may have helped hold them in the area, keeping at bay any urges they might have had to strike north again to look for signs of home. This unique jump start, accented by breeding activity in the first year, may have been the single most important factor in the program's early success.

As if suits by the Sierra Club Legal Defense Fund and Farm Bureau weren't enough, thrown into the mix at the same time was legal action from a couple in Wyoming, who maintained that because wolves inhabited Yellowstone all along, the reintroduction was unnecessary. These previous resident wolves, the couple suggested, had escaped detection by researchers for twenty years by employing some highly unusual behaviors, including refusing to howl, not traveling in packs, and steering clear of roads and trails. In truth biologists have been remarkably successful detecting wolf packs in locations around the world. Yet beginning with a landmark study by biologist John Weaver in the mid-1970s, no one ever managed to find a viable population of wolves in greater Yellowstone. It was in drawing from this work that Weaver became among the first to recommend wolf reintroduction in a report to the National Park Service in 1978.[1] While the argument of stealth wolf packs never made much legal headway, in the end it was the wolves themselves who settled the matter. No one, after all, is better at finding wolves than other wolves. When our reintroduced animals dispersed—all of them, by the way, wearing radio collars—traveling alone across hundreds of miles for months at a time, often on the lookout for potential mates, not a single one ever managed to hook up with an uncollared, non-reintroduced wolf.

Even though this was one of the last legal actions claiming wolves were already in Yellowstone, an ongoing complaint even today is that the wolves we reintroduced are significantly different from those of the past—specifically, that we took from Canada a larger, more aggressive subspecies. Yet modern genetic analyses of wolves living across North America doesn't support such claims. Wolves travel far and wide, and because of this they don't tend to readily segregate out, grouping into different subpopulations. In other words, their wide-ranging movements tend to keep the gene pool mixed, which in turn prevents the creation of localized forms.[2] It's largely for this reason that over the years modern taxonomic analyses have reduced the number of wolf subspecies from twenty-four, to just five.[3] Only when we take a wolf from the northern end of their range, in the Arctic, and compare them to a wolf from the southern end, in Mexico, are we able to discern a noticeable difference. And even then such differences are subtle. An Arctic wolf, for example, would have no trouble breeding successfully with a Mexican wolf.

At their worst, these ongoing notions of a super-subspecies have been downright macabre. One frequently heard campfire tale is that Yellowstone's reintroduced wolves "kill for fun," engaging in such bizarre behavior as chewing the lips off elk, leaving the rest to rot. Such stories are grim reminders that no animal on the face of the earth has had a more vigorous blanket of mythology laid on it than the wolf. Granted, some ancient cultures, not to mention many contemporary indigenous people, have long told stories painting the wolf in glowing terms. At times he appears as a pillar of wisdom, standing now and then with "brother" coyote, who by contrast is depicted as clever but self-defeating. Positive wolf hero figures are not only accomplished at survival, procuring food and defending territory, but are often seen as a kind of model for human social order. The fact that wolves are highly independent, for instance, yet at the same time fiercely loyal to the pack, represented a behavioral ideal to cultures who valued both individual freedoms and social responsibility. Likewise, the extraordinary dedication wolves show in caring for pups, with virtually every adult in the pack engaged in those duties from roughly May to September, was hardly lost on the native tribes who shared the land with them.

But on the other side of wolf lore are found tales dark and murky and filled with fear, causing angst right into modern times. They are stories spun out across nearly a thousand years, catching fire in the Middle Ages, when the Catholic Church voted the wolf as "the devil's dog"—literal proof of evil on the earth. And while that may have been highly effective for arousing the faithful it did little for the wolf, what with his reputation already fading as declining prey populations forced him to dine ever more frequently on livestock. During this era wolves were routinely either burned at the stake or hung by the neck in village squares.

First in Europe, and later in the United States, wolves were wiped out with a vengeance applied to no other animal on earth. "Wolfers," as American hunters were often called, went far beyond the usual killing tools of rifles, snare traps, and cyanide baits. Many staked steel wires near den sites, attaching to the free ends large fish hooks wrapped with pieces of chicken. Pups coming out of the den at night swallowed the morsels whole, sometimes literally pulling their stomachs out trying to get loose. Others gobbled hunks of meat laced with razor blades and nails, or in some cases were set on fire. Once captured some had their lower jaws cut off or wired shut, later released to slowly starve to death. Half a century later, soldiers returning from World War II quickly took up the sport of shooting wolves in northern Minnesota and Michigan, referring to the activity as "killing Nazis." (As an interesting aside, wolf hunters in the early twentieth century routinely laced the carcasses of wolf-killed prey with strychnine. When the animals returned for a second round of feeding, which is typical wolf behavior, they were of course killed. In a remarkably short amount of time some animals adopted new feeding habits, no longer returning to a carcass after the initial kill. Far from earning respect for being smart, people began accusing them of wasting meat, of killing for fun.)

What is it that makes wolves ripe for such hatred and cruelty? After all, other animals are clearly more ferocious, more dangerous to humans, from bears to lions to rattlesnakes. Over the past hundred years in all of North America there have been less than twenty cases of wolves attacking humans, not one of which has resulted in a fatality.[4] And while it's true that these other predators—"stenchy beasts," as they were commonly referred to in the Middle Ages—were also greatly disliked, none has ever been given the weight of evil itself. Was it, as Rolf Peterson suggests, that wolves are so similar to us—adaptable, dedicated to mates, relying on a cooperative social structure—that puts such a chill in our spines? Or have our nightmares about seeing the devil in the eyes of the wolf been merely bad dreams about our own animal nature?

Considering this tortured past, combined with the honest-to-goodness trouble that wolves do occasionally get into, it's not surprising that the Yellowstone reintroduction would draw anxious, even bitter responses. A mere decade ago there were people living on the edges of this ecosystem who refused to let their children stand outside and wait for the school bus, convinced they might be carried off by wolves. Many influential politicians continue to demand wolf death in no uncertain terms. So great has the frenzy been at times that one day recovery coordinator Ed Bangs—the man in charge of all wolf decisions in the Northern Rocky Mountains—told me soberly that it was now clear to him how people had come to burn witches.

Given these fiery feelings, security around this project during the reintroduction phase was extremely tight. Whether we were in Canada or Yellowstone or anywhere in-between the wolves were never without armed law officers standing nearby—twenty-four hours a day, seven days a week. While in the acclimation pens specially trained security rangers were on hand, though not actually in view, since we didn't want to accustom the animals to humans. These security forces never appeared when I and other biologists were in the pens feeding the wolves, but we always knew they were out there, watching our every move.

Yet for all this bad blood, people who admire the wolf make a tremendous mistake when they ignore the very real problems it can create—when they fail to separate noble ideas of the animal from the reality on the ground. There will always be a small number of wolves willing to add beef or lamb to their diet. For ranchers, the loss of even a single cow or sheep can be significant—not merely because many cattle operations operate on razor-thin margins of profit, but because for many it's more than a little disturbing to see an animal you helped bring into the world being served up as dinner for a bunch of predators. What's more, much of the apprehension about wolves was handed down to locals from their own relatives, many of whom really did face significant ordeals, especially around the turn of the twentieth century. What's seldom understood, though, is that a majority of those problems stemmed from the fact that unregulated hunting had sent the prey base plummeting to its lowest levels in history. Not just wolves, but cougars, coyotes, and even bears were heading for ranch lands. On the other hand, by the time wolves were being reintroduced to Yellowstone sound conservation efforts—many initiated during the early decades of the twentieth century—had led to historic high levels of many prey populations, including elk. In truth, an ongoing challenge for Wyoming and Montana in recent years has been figuring out how to reduce elk herds, more often than not by liberalizing hunting activity.

Finally landing in Yellowstone with wolves in tow, in January of 1995, marked the end of two decades of extraordinarily difficult work. Countless hours had been invested by biologists and land managers, by dozens of politicians and thousands of citizens, both in this region and around the country. The wolf had come home to the world's first national park. And the place would never again be quite the same.

Portrait of a Wolf

NUMBER 9

The remarkable story of wolf Number 9 begins when she and her yearling daughter, Number 7, were captured on a bitterly cold day in Alberta. From there they began the long journey to Yellowstone, finally landing in an acclimation pen in the Lamar Valley, not far from the famed Buffalo Ranch, near a small stream called Rose Creek. About a week later mother and daughter were joined in the pen by another adult wolf, an especially bold and beautiful animal known as Number 10—the sole member of his pack to have been caught in Canada. Given that these two adults were strangers, we weren't at all sure how things were going to go between them. Actually, the relationship got off to a rocky start, with 10 nipping 9 on several occasions hard enough to draw blood—his way, we believe, of making it very clear who was in charge of the show.

As the days went by, though, to our enormous relief things improved between the pair, at least to the point where they were able to ignore each other. From there things got better still; during times of rest the two animals began curling up in the pen, getting ever closer. Though we weren't aware of it at the time, 9 and 10 would actually end up mating—something we didn't think would happen in any of the acclimation pens, let alone one containing two adults that started off as complete strangers. Sadly, 10 was not long for this world. Yet the wolf he made peace with, and then finally bred, would prove one of the most critical players in all of Yellowstone. Genetic studies done in 1999 showed that 79 percent of all wolves in Yellowstone—including several others of great importance—were related to the outstanding alpha female Number 9.

On walking out of the acclimation pen in March of 1995, the three wolves stayed together for only a week before 9's yearling daughter, Number 7, split off to begin a life of her own. During a routine tracking flight on April 18 we managed to locate her well to the west, near Tower Junction; her mother and Number 10, though, were nowhere to be found, vanishing like snow on spring ground. Eleven long, anxious days passed before we managed to find them again—forty miles to the northeast at the edge of the Great Plains, on the pine-covered flanks of Mount Maurice. Shortly afterward magnificent Number 10 was dead, shot down on a sage-covered hill by a man who claimed he thought it was a wild dog. Number 10 would be the first of the Yellowstone wolves to die. Because he was the first to go, but also because he was such a splendid animal, I took it hard, as did a lot of other people both inside and outside the wolf project.

At the time of the shooting Number 9 was five miles to the south, wandering in a tight circle on the west flank of Mount Maurice, waiting, watching through the timber for a mate that would never return. Wolves show a fantastic degree of loyalty to other members of their pack, especially their mates, often hooking up for life. In that sense Number 10's failure to appear would've surely caused 9 great anxiety. The fact that she wasn't moving much—leading a somewhat sedentary lifestyle, roaming the same small area on Mount Maurice over and over—suggested to us that either she was injured or about to den. To find out we launched a ground search, led by U.S. Fish and Wildlife biologist Joe Fontaine. Working closely with the indefatigable Carter Niemeyer, Joe was eventually able to find a litter of pups under a tree, the whole bunch knotted together in a big ball of fur. Not wanting to keep 9 away from her pups a minute longer than necessary, Fontaine made a hasty retreat. Piecing the story together, we came to understand that when 9 couldn't wait any longer for her mate she'd hurriedly scraped a shallow depression in the ground under a large Douglas fir, then laid down on her side with her back against the trunk, giving birth to the first sizable litter of pups born in the greater Yellowstone ecosystem in some seventy years.

Unlike some mammals, wolves aren't at all inclined to play the single-parent role. A lone female like 9 would be hard-pressed to leave the den site for food without placing the pups at risk from predators ranging from cougars to coyotes to stray dogs. With that dismal fact staring us in the face, there began a heated debate among wolf recovery team members. Some in the U.S. Fish and Wildlife Service (the agency actually responsible for 9 and her pups, given that they were now located outside Yellowstone National Park) were inclined to let nature take its course. After all, they maintained, these were wild animals, and should be managed as such. The National Park Service team, meanwhile, led at that time by the feisty director of the wolf project, Mike Phillips, couldn't imagine leaving these miracle pups—offspring we never expected to see in this first year—to end up as lunch for some coyote. Better to gather them up and take them by helicopter back to the Rose Creek pen, he argued, releasing them when they were bigger, more able to fend for themselves. It was a spirited argument, but in the end the nod went to Mike Phillips. We wasted little time launching a capture plan.

Which is how on May 17 I found myself at the south edge of Red Lodge, leaning out an upstairs window of the Super 8 Motel with a radio antenna in my hand, listening for Number 9 to trip the modified leg hold traps we'd laid for her near where Joe Fontaine had seen those pups. Hour after hour dragged by with no action—not all that surprising, given how routinely wolves manage to evade traps set for them. In the end, though, in the wee hours before dawn 9 finally took the bait, drawn to one trap set by Carter Niemeyer, containing scat from her now deceased partner.

And still the emotional roller coaster continued. Having finally caught and processed Number 9, checking her health and then placing her, still sedated, in a kennel in the shade, we headed off to gather her pups, assuming they were under that same tree where Fontaine had spotted them a week before. We found the tree, lifted up the low-hanging branches, and to our utter shock, discovered every single pup was gone. If over the past ten years there've been moments close to terrifying, this was one of them. Should we fail to find the pups we'd of course have to let 9 go, and the chances of catching her a second time were slim to none. Checking maps and photographs from previous tracking flights we noted an area up the mountain a good three-quarters of a mile where she'd been pinpointed on several other occasions. Against slim odds the team spread out and began moving upslope, each of us imitating the quiet grunting sound that adult wolves often make when returning to the den, hoping to draw out the pups. Luck was on our side. After a long search they finally betrayed their location high on the mountain in a jumble of rocks, calling out in squeaks and squeals. As near as we can tell Fontaine's earlier visit had worried the alpha female, leading her to move them one by one—probably under the cover of a dark night— from that original scrape of dirt to this more secure location.

Pulling wolf pups from a jumble of rocks is no easy proposition; even at three weeks we expected these little fur balls to put up a fight. Slowly, carefully we fished seven of them out of the talus slide, each one moaning and growling. At that point I felt sure we had the whole bunch, but Carter and Joe weren't convinced, thinking there might be one more deep in the rocks, hunkered at the back of a dark crevice I couldn't quite get to. Again and again I strained to stuff my six-foot, two-inch frame into that crack far enough to reach the back of the hole, but all I could touch—and this just with the end of my middle finger—was something that felt more like a piece of mud than a wolf pup. I needed two more inches. Luckily our helicopter pilot had a folding pair of pliers, and armed with these back in I went, Carter and Joe at my legs pushing excitedly to get me farther into the rocks, leaving a fair collection of bruises in the process. Finally, at the limit of my reach I was able to get ahold of that solid mass with the pliers, then slowly pulled it out. Lo and behold, there was the eighth and final wolf pup. Breathing an enormous sigh of relief we loaded the family into the helicopter and flew them back to Yellowstone. In the course of my week-by-week, year-by-year tracking flights I've often wondered whether or not that pup is still alive— whether, even, he was in fact the future alpha male Number 21 of the Druid Peak Pack. Having helped effect his rescue I have to admit to feeling a certain connection to him. But like so much having to do with Yellowstone's wolves, I'll never know.

I wish I could say that after the rescue nothing else happened to stress either the wolves or us. But having transported the family safely back to Yellowstone, in late July a windstorm blew in and nearly destroyed the pen, some ten trees ripping through the chain link. Shortly afterward, every single pup scampered away. Number 9, though—ever the wary wolf—decided against escape, and on the day I arrived to feed she was still inside the pen. It was easy to see the pups frolicking just outside the enclosure, but catching them was another matter. At one point I nearly knocked myself senseless making a dive with an outstretched net trying to catch one of the little ones, who easily—and, it seemed, with great joy—simply outran me. In the end we got six of them, the other two remaining at large, roaming freely but never going far from their family. One of those little renegades, Number 18, lived to be eight years old and for many years was the alpha female of the Rose Creek II Pack (the Rose Creek group had a "II" added to their pack name at the point there were no longer any of the original members). Appropriately, she was never collared, remaining through 2003 the only alpha female in all of Yellowstone we couldn't capture during our yearly collaring efforts. Luckily, her markings were distinctive enough to allow us to at least observe her from the air.

Number 9 and her pups—those we could catch, anyway—remained confined for another nine weeks, until the end of hunting season on the national forest lands adjacent to the park. Even with the pups much older and larger, fully able to travel, we had no illusions about the pack's chances of success. Number 9 was still the sole skilled hunter and defender, able to kill game but unlikely to be able to protect her pups from attacks by other packs. Besides, autumn is no easy time for wolves. It's then that prey animals have a clear edge, having been fattened and strengthened by a summer of good eating. But on October 11, the day we headed in to free the wolves by removing a panel from the pen (we were no longer cutting holes in the chain-link, thus saving on pen parts), suddenly the odds got a lot better. In a fine turn of events a lone wolf from the Crystal Pack—Number 8, who the week before had been fifteen miles away near the Grand Canyon of the Yellowstone—showed up at the pen site in a courting mood, unable to resist the attraction of a lone female. It was a match made in heaven. Number 8 received a big promotion to alpha wolf, while 9 got a much-needed hunting partner. Meanwhile the eight youngsters had a father figure who they welcomed with no questions asked, nipping and barking and pulling on his tail with abandon. This willingness to adopt offspring sired by other animals, though common in wolves, is in the mammal world actually a rare quality. One of these male pups, 21, besides becoming alpha male of the Druid Pack, would himself adopt five youngsters, sired by wolf Number 38.

The group was a family now, with the alpha pair going on to produce pups in every year from 1996 through 1999. Number 9 would breed yet again in 2000, though none of her pups survived, perhaps in part because of her advanced years. No one knows the maximum breeding age for a female wolf, but by that point she was likely eight or even nine, clearly pushing the limit; her black fur had turned so gray that from a distance it appeared nearly white. That spring she disappeared east of the park, in the rugged folds of the Absaroka Wilderness. Her radio signal was never heard again. There have been no sightings, no tracks. Even now I get calls and e-mails from people wanting to know if it's possible to start a fund to erect a statue somewhere in the park to honor her extraordinary life. As for her second mate, Number 8, he too thrived, remaining the alpha male of the Rose Creek Pack until 2000. Not long after his death there began a long, slow decline for the Rose Creek wolves, suggesting his influence may have been greater than we ever realized.

Five of the eight pups born from the famous pairing of 9 and 10 would themselves go on to breed, including females 16, 17, 18, and 19. Number 18—the little pup who refused to be caught outside that damaged acclimation pen, and who likewise remained uncaptured as an alpha female—would in 1997 breed in the same pack as her mother, each female setting up at a separate den site. The following year both mother and daughter bred again, this time, remarkably, wriggling in and out of the same den—behavior seldom seen outside Yellowstone. That may have been too much family for one little house, though, since the next spring each wolf again secured her own site. When 9 actually left the pack the next spring, abandoning her alpha position, 18 moved in to fill the slot. Number 18 bred both in that year and again in 2001, ultimately giving birth to some thirty-two pups. Throughout the period she seemed content using the same nooks and crannies of the territory she'd first learned about from her mother.

Meanwhile her sister, Number 19, didn't fare half as well. Soon after giving birth alone near Slough Creek she was killed, likely in a territorial skirmish by members of the neighboring Druid Peak Pack; her pups, suddenly orphaned, would all die at roughly two weeks old at the den where they were born. (Their bodies were later retrieved, and can now be seen in an interpretive display at Yellowstone's Albright Visitor Center.) Nor was fate particularly kind to another sister, Number 17, the only gray in a litter of black pups. After hooking up with male Number 34, in July of 1997 she too would die—less than three months after giving birth to pups—the result of a stick piercing her in the chest while on a furious chase of an elk. Suddenly finding himself a single father, Number 34 traveled some thirty miles with the little ones to the den site of his former mate's sister, Number 16. They stayed together for a while, yet in the end trouble befell this female as well when a car struck her and broke her leg—an injury that kept her from returning and caring for the pups. Despite our best efforts to offer food, all of them eventually perished. Number 16's leg did eventually heal, though, at which point she was right back in the action, going on to pair with wolf Number 165 north of the park to form the Sheep Mountain Pack, giving birth to pups in both 1998 and 1999.

If fortune was hard on some of 9's daughters, it was somewhat kinder to the one son who managed to survive to breeding age, Number 21. After two-and-a-half years spent with his mother and the rest of the Rose Creek Pack, he left that group to become alpha male of Druid Peak, gaining the top dog position in December of 1997 under rather unfortunate circumstances. In that era, probably because they were still settling into the landscape, the Druid Peak animals sometimes traveled onto prime elk hunting areas on national forest lands just east of the park. On one such ill-fated trip the only two adult males of the pack were cut down by poachers' bullets—including alpha male Number 38, a particularly strong and beautiful animal. This shooting, which didn't actually kill 38 outright, led us into a hearty debate about whether or not we should intervene and tend his wounds. We decided against it, though in truth I've often wondered about that choice, especially since I was the one with the grisly task of tracking 38 while he slowly died—a process that took eleven days. The job was hardly a challenge, given that the bullet wound rendered him unable to move very far on any given day. Despite our earlier decision to "let nature take its course," we eventually tried slipping him some meat, but he never took it. In the end he died from a combination of his wounds, and quite likely starvation. Indeed, the same wolf that had tipped the scales at a hearty 125 pounds at the time of the shooting, would by his death weigh a scant 88 pounds.

In his newfound role as alpha male, 21 was not only responsible for a great many litters—fathering pups seven years running, from 1998 through 2004—but for a long time was one of the most easily seen and often celebrated of all Yellowstone's wolves. Carrying the same large shoulders that distinguished his mother, 21's profile, even from a distance, was hard to mistake. Also like his mother he was a black wolf that grayed over time, giving him a distinct coloration. He was remarkably gentle. Many a time did he come back from a hunt only to be mobbed by twenty pups begging for food. He took it calmly, though, always in stride. Likewise, after making a kill he was never seen fiercely defending the carcass from underlings, forcing them to wait their turn, as is so often assumed to be the case with wolves. Instead he would sometimes simply walk away—to urinate, maybe even take a nap—allowing young wolves who had nothing to do with the kill to take their fill. Likewise, when tussling with underlings he would now and then take a playful posture, letting the youngsters be on top of him, as a father might do when wrestling with his young sons.[1] For all these reasons, 21 became for many of the Lamar Valley wildlife fans the favorite wolf of them all.

CHAPTER 3

A PARADISE CALLED
YELLOWSTONE

From at least the days when trapper Osborne Russell
first stumbled into the Lamar Valley in 1835 (he knew it
as Secluded Valley), lost in a reverie of what it would be like to
spend the rest of his life wrapped in such wild, unfettered beauty—
"where happiness and contentment seemed to reign in wild roman-
tic splendor"—travelers have been swooning over this magnificent
landscape. In this toss of fescue and sticky geranium and sage, cut

by the easy drift of an icy mountain river, visitors are afforded glimpses of an American West nearly unchanged from the glories of two hundred years ago. Lying at the heart of what biologists refer to as the northern range, here is home ground for coyote and bald eagle, bison and prong-horn. Even bighorn sheep and mountain goats can be seen now and then clinging to the steep terrain that rims the valley. And in winter, one of the world's largest, densest elk herds imaginable, which a decade ago was coming down from a historic high of some twenty thousand animals. It was here that the last wolf disappeared from Yellowstone, killed in 1926. And here that three groups of reintroduced wolves would in 1995 once more walk into the life of the wild, taking their pack names from natural features laid down on maps long before: Crystal Creek, Rose Creek, and Soda Butte.

The extraordinary prey base embodied by this elk herd was a driving factor in determining where in Canada we'd go to capture wolves bound for Yellowstone. Simply put, we wanted animals used to hunting not caribou or moose, but rather Rocky Mountain elk—the same prey that would make up the bulk of their food supply in and around the national park. The vast majority of wolves hunt what their parents teach them to hunt, avoiding animals not familiar to them—using a so-called "search image."[1] As pointed out by livestock industry spokesman Wallis Huidekoper, speaking to the annual convention of the Montana Stock Growers Association in 1916, "It is a well-known fact that stock-killing individuals among wolves are only a small proportion of their kind inhabiting a given area." To be sure, there will always be found the occasional maverick willing to take on unfamiliar prey, including cows or sheep. Often these are fairly young wolves, yearlings ("teenagers," if you will), eager to try something new. What's more, wolves are keen observational learners, able to change behavior simply by watching fellow pack members. That means bad habits can spread quickly through the group. Still, this is the exception, not the rule.

With the top predator missing from Yellowstone for some seventy years, there had evolved in the region's elk herds a higher-than-normal percentage of older, weaker animals.[2] Indeed, necropsies done on wolf kills in the northern part of the park between 1995 and 2005 showed the average age of adult cow elk taken by wolves as fourteen years old, with animals twenty or older not uncommon. What's more, high densities of elk and other ungulates living at or near the threshold of what the available food resource can sustain—a number referred to as "carrying capacity"—are far more likely to suffer from poor nutrition. That, in turn, renders them relatively easy prey. From a purely biological point of view, then, the timing of the reintroduction was perfect—a fact made abundantly clear within hours of the wolves walking free of their acclimation pens. The Soda Butte Pack made a quick kill a mere half mile from their fenced enclosure, as did that highly confident Rose Creek wolf, Number 10, who just a few hundred yards from his pen managed to kill a bull elk weakened by winter and poor nutrition.

Given all that was in the wolves' favor, some people wondered about our decision in Yellowstone to first place them in acclimation pens—chain-link enclosures roughly an acre in size, where the animals spent their first ten weeks in the national park. (The use of such enclosures prior to release—termed a "soft release"—may seem especially curious given that no such pens were used in the Idaho segment of the wolf reintroduction. There animals were instead launched by means of "hard release," which means they were delivered to a site, one to a kennel, then the doors opened to send them hustling off into the wild.)

The reason for using soft release in Yellowstone has to do with how close the national park is to cattle and sheep ranches. Wolves have a strong homing response. If you capture and later turn them loose in a strange place their first reaction is to head off in the direction they came from, sometimes traveling forty miles or more, looking for familiar landmarks—signs of home. Had Yellowstone's wolves headed north thirty or forty miles from their release sites in the Lamar Valley, they would've found themselves right in the middle of livestock country—something we wanted to avoid at all costs. The pens were an attempt to soften, or attenuate, this strong behavioral response. By all indication it worked, as few wolves ever ventured very far north out of the park.

For the team of wolf project employees, maintenance workers, and volunteers who in 1994 and '95 helped build what would eventually become seven pens—pounding steel posts, ratcheting enormous panels into place—it often felt as if we were erecting maximum-security detention centers. Ten-foot-high runs of chain-link were capped by inward-leaning aprons, the corners of the enclosure rounded to guard against wolves climbing up and out. To keep the animals from digging out, four-foot-wide mats of chain-link were laid along the inside perimeter of the pens, staked down every four feet with long spikes of iron rebar.

Of course during their time spent in the pens the wolves had to be tended to, which meant twice-weekly feedings of road-killed deer, elk, moose, and bison. In the fall prior to the wolves' arrival state and county agencies alerted us to fatally wounded animals on the region's highways. The word was passed on to the wolf project, as often as not to volunteers Deb Guernsey and Carrie Schaefer, who then sped off in a pickup truck to retrieve the bodies—a job that earned them the somewhat dubious title of "carcass queens." It was smelly, inglorious work, followed by the equally tedious job of gutting the animals before storing them in freezers for later use. Given all the threats being made against wolves at that time we never talked much about any of this, afraid someone might start lacing the roadkill with strychnine.

Because the pens were located anywhere from a quarter-mile to a full mile from the nearest plowed road, getting several hundred pounds of meat in each week was no easy task. With snow on the ground we relied on mule-drawn sleighs—a means of transportation that meant bringing in area cowboys to serve as mule-drivers, men who for the

48

most part were strongly opposed to wolf reintroduction. Yet they did an extraordinary job, often under trying conditions, including dealing with several Park Service mules with quirky dispositions. Two of those mules, for instance, while hooked to the sleigh seemed to take great delight in running over whoever was trying to steady them. In addition to sleighs we occasionally used packhorses, and every now and then even carried meat in on our backs. I recall one day doing exactly that in full Park Service uniform with Hillary Clinton along; all of a sudden the elk leg I was carrying started leaking blood all over my back, giving the First Lady what was no doubt a less-than-inspiring sight.

Some people worried that all these trips to the pens for feeding would habituate the wolves to humans. But as one who made a lot of those trips, I ended up thinking much the opposite was true. Food in hand or not, the wolves clearly didn't like us anywhere near them. Given that the pen curtailed their normal flight response, my sense was that the enclosure may have actually reinforced their fear of humans. Either way, it's worth noting that following their release it would be several years before we recorded a Yellowstone wolf getting anywhere close to a human.

Yet the use of acclimation pens was hardly perfect. If ever there's been an animal that loves freedom it's the wolf, and several did everything they could to get out—not just digging and chewing on the fence, but sometimes hanging by their teeth from the overhangs. This we considered a big deal. A wolf makes her living by her teeth, after all, and we worried constantly that worn-down or broken canines might limit an animal's ability to hunt—aging the wolf, in a sense, before her time. Hours were spent at the wolf office in Mammoth concocting schemes to stop the chewing—repellents, electric fencing, even giant Plexiglas liners. None, though, proved practical. Thankfully most of the wolves didn't chew, and even those that did usually stopped after a few weeks.

There was one big exception—a group captured from British Columbia during the second year of the project, in 1996, first penned and finally released near Nez Perce Creek, in the central region of the national park. The Nez Perce wolves, as they were known, never really settled into the acclimation pen. Some people speculated their restlessness was due to the pen being located within earshot of snowmobiles, a sound that in Canada they would've almost certainly associated with the men who hunted them through the long months of winter. Still another theory was that their unsettledness had been inspired by a single alpha female, Number 27. A fence biter from the very beginning, this was one wolf seriously unhappy about captivity. (Nor for that matter was she particularly fond of me. One day while feeding I walked toward her with an elk leg and, unlike every other wolf I encountered during the reintroduction, she didn't give ground. Pausing at a distance of about ten feet we both stood fast, looking at each other. Just as I was thinking about taking one last step to assert myself, I heard a deep, guttural growl coming from her throat. I decided against the extra step.)

During the first round of wolf releases, when time came to open the pen gates and turn the animals into the wild, to our surprise most of them refused to leave. This was exactly opposite of what we'd expected, having figured we'd be dashing off at a good clip just to stay out of their way. While to us the situation was frustrating, others found it mildly amusing—or in a couple cases, even pathetic. Conservative commentator Paul Harvey announced one day to his radio show audience that by feeding the wolves for ten weeks we had turned them into welfare animals, too fond of government handouts to ever go out and make a living on their own. But through telephone consultations with other wolf biologists, including Dave Mech, Rolf Peterson, Ed Bangs, and Steve Fritts, we came to believe that our passing through the pen gates some twenty times in the previous two-and-a-half months, carting in several tons of carcass meat, had caused the wolves to see the opening not as a portal to freedom, but as a dangerous link to humans. They may well starve to death, suggested Mech, before they'd walk into a part of the pen with such strong associations to humans.

We thought it might be possible to solve this problem by cutting a hole somewhere else in the pen, near those places in the enclosure where the animals had found comfort during their long internment— places marked by well-worn tracks in the snow from frequent pacing, as well as hollow depressions where they'd bedded down to rest. It worked. Yet even after these new holes were cut the wolves tended to be cautious, not leaving until long after we'd disappeared. Not so with wolf Number 27. Being especially bold she dashed out of the freshly cut escape hole in full view of the research team, her three daughters running for her heels, trying their best to catch up. From Nez Perce Creek she headed north, covering some twenty-five miles every night, often through deep snow, leaving even those of us in the tracking plane hard pressed to keep tabs on her. In the end her three young daughters got their fill of this brutal pace, finally breaking off to travel by themselves. Meanwhile her mate, along with a male pup, waited a full day before leaving the acclimation pen; by then her trail had gone cold, making it impossible to catch her.

In was probably Interstate 90 that finally turned her, sending her drifting back toward the rugged folds of the Beartooths, where she'd eventually give birth to pups near the tiny town of Nye, Montana— unfortunately, smack in the middle of sheep and cattle country. Her proximity to livestock, along with the fact that she was a single mother, led us to launch a capture operation to bring her back to the Nez Perce pen and release her later in the year. Number 27, though, had other ideas. Proving yet again not just the wariness of wolves, but also their astonishing intelligence, over and over she gave us the slip—all through summer, through autumn and then into winter, until one bone-chilling day in February we finally managed to dart her from a helicopter and fly her back to the national park.

Meanwhile Number 48, the one remaining pup from a litter born in the spring of 1996, seemed to have taken escape lessons from mom, remaining at-large for another three weeks. Unfortunately, when we did finally catch up to 48 it was after a sheep-killing incident. Following the "two strikes you're out" rule of the day, whereby wolves who preyed on livestock a second time were eliminated (these days, with a larger population, the rule has been hardened to "one strike and you're out"), we carted her back to the park and placed her in the pen with her mother and pack mates, hoping we could prevent her from getting into trouble a second time. Thankfully, the rehabilitation took hold. Number 48 went on to become alpha female of the Nez Perce Pack, a position that as of this writing she continues to hold, the group ranging through the national park between Old Faithful, Hayden Valley, and Madison Junction. When we last captured her for a collar replacement in November 2003, I noticed she'd taken on the traits of an old wolf—ears tattered, a graying face and muzzle.

As the time approached to release Number 27 we were holding our breath, wondering what sort of goose chase she might have in store for us this time. In the early weeks, though, she stayed put, probably in part because her daughter had had a litter of pups of her own; like most adult females, 27 was likely unwilling to leave, wanting to do her part in the "extended child care" that's such a mainstay of wolf society. Now made up of three generations, the pack slowly but surely moved across the park, traveling from one camp to another, finally landing north of Yellowstone Lake in the magnificent Hayden Valley. These base camps, known as rendezvous sites, are a kind of aboveground den—secure and secluded, perfect for stashing pups when they're still too young to do much traveling. From these sites adults take turns hunting, bringing back nourishment for the young either as pieces of carcass or as food in their stomachs, while the rest of the group remains close by to watch over and play with the pups, spending hours enduring mock ambushes and having their tails yanked by some of the most playful, insistent children of the animal world. For those of us who follow wolves, sorting out pups is always an easy task. Most youngsters can't manage a dozen steps before falling out of line and jumping into the air, as if firecrackers were exploding under their feet.

Pups do grow up, of course, by fall gaining enough maturity to travel with the older members of the pack. Soon Number 27 was off and running again—this time heading west, landing some fifty miles away near Dillon, Montana. Shortly afterward we got the news we'd feared all along: sheep were dead in the area, and by all appearances 27 had something to do with it. This being her second offense, in October a helicopter took off from Dillon, Montana, with a gunner on board. Thirty minutes later, the great wanderer was dead.

To be honest, 27's death gave me pause. She'd always shown the kind of independent streak that spoke of the wild, unfettered heart that wolves are both loved and hated for. I often imagined that we of the wolf project were to her nothing but a rotten nuisance, creatures intent on disrupting her desire to simply live in the wilderness on her own terms. As mentioned earlier, she growled at me one day in the Nez Perce pen—not something most wolves ever did. Beyond that, though, before we actually brought her to the Nez Perce site after that capture near Nye, Montana, we placed her alone for a short time in another holding facility, near Fishing Bridge. On the day we went into that pen to capture her for transport to the Nez Perce site, she lunged through waist-deep snow ahead of our nets, finally stopping to face us, teeth bared and growling. In that face, grizzled and gray with age, was the look of a beautifully fierce and resolute animal. The only wolf skull I have in my office in Mammoth is that of 27—a reminder of her incorrigible, incorruptible spirit.

The wolves with her at the time of her death, including her son, Number 29, were brought back to the Nez Perce acclimation pen for what was hoped to be a serious bout of rehabilitation. But Number 29 would keep alive the memory of his mother—in particular, her distaste for the Nez Perce pen—by applying some pretty clever tricks of his own. Of the thirty-one Canadian wolves reintroduced to Yellowstone during 1995 and 1996, Number 29 would have the distinction of becoming the only wolf to figure out how to escape from the acclimation pens. For the longest time we were clueless, hugely embarrassed by the thought that we'd placed him and his pack mates in a pen with a hole in it. Over and over we walked the enclosure, failing to find any flaw. Unlike his mother, rather than bolting once he was free of the pen this little escape artist instead set about digging back under the fence to free his mates, at which point the whole gang took off for Dillon, where we had to recapture them. Desperate to hold these Houdinis we decided to fortify the pen with an electric fence, only to have him give us the slip yet again.

Following this final jailbreak, the U.S. Fish and Wildlife Service told us that given the group's history of getting into trouble with livestock, if 29 and his mates left the park again they'd be shot at the border. On the other hand, if they behaved for a year the slate would be wiped clean. This seriously affected our approach to dealing with the pack, making us decide against capturing them the following winter for radio collaring for fear that it might cause them to range far afield—even though no data exists to suggest that it would. Besides, my bosses were strongly opposed to stressing them in any way. On one hand they didn't want to risk the safety of the animals. At the same time, if the wolves did decide to leave the park they didn't want people blaming the collaring operation for their departure. On making this last great escape Number 29 headed not west but south, where for a time he joined up with other wolves, eventually becoming one of the founding members of the Gros Ventre Pack near Jackson, Wyoming. One day in the pen, long after 29 was gone, I happened to look up and see a small tuft of hair hanging high on the chain-link. Suddenly I got it. Incredibly, he'd jumped up ten feet to the overhanging panel at the top of the enclosure, dangling there by his teeth, pawing the air like a monkey until he was finally able to find purchase and scramble out.

It was a trick with serious consequences. The last time I handled 29 his canine teeth were all but gone, broken off to stubs during those inspired athletic moments hanging from the chain-link. Again, given that wolves make their living with their teeth we worried that when it came to taking down elk he'd be severely compromised. But that didn't seem to be the case. Over the years I've asked several wolf biologists how this animal could still function while missing the teeth responsible for grabbing, holding, and tearing the flesh of his prey. The usual answer is that the sheer force of a wolf's jaw would by itself be enough to do the job—a force, by the way, with a crushing power of more than twelve hundred pounds per square inch (compared to roughly six hundred pounds per square inch for a large dog).[3] Number 29 may have been reliant on other wolves from his pack to open up a freshly killed elk, tearing through the tough hide, but once that was done he could use the shearing action of his premolars and molars—carnassial teeth, unique to carnivores—to consume the prey. Then again, some of Number 29's success may have had to do with simple determination. In my twenty-five years studying wolves they never cease to impress me with how they almost never give up. I imagined 29 chasing and killing elk with his bum teeth as if nothing had changed at all.

Now firmly established on the west side of Yellowstone National Park, the Nez Perce wolves still show some of the old fondness for wandering. Having collared new members of the pack in subsequent years, we know they leave the park in winter, traveling widely, one time in early 2003 showing up on the National Elk Refuge near Jackson, Wyoming. Sooner or later they always return, though, led by old Number 48, sometimes the entire group traveling together and at other times individual members dropping off to go their separate ways. Despite such flux the core group is still intact, for the most part occupying the very heart of the territory that Number 27 fled back in 1996. In some years theirs has been the largest pack in the park, exceeding twenty animals.

If many of us with the wolf project tend to recall the early Nez Perce wolves for how they routinely exhausted us, they were a paid vacation compared to another group placed in this same pen in late 1996—wolves not a part of the original animals brought down from Canada. In the fall of that year two alpha wolves from northwest Montana, near the town of Choteau—members of what was known in the area as the Sawtooth Pack—had been found killing cows. As a result they were removed from the population, making orphans of their ten pups. Not wanting to leave these youngsters in the field, where their lack of experience would almost surely doom them, we agreed to take them in here at Yellowstone. Personally I was uneasy with that decision, doubtful we'd be able to integrate the pups successfully into our existing population. But we made our best effort, placing them in a pen with two adult Nez Perce wolves in confinement for rehabilitation.

While in the pen everyone seemed to get along famously. Yet on release in March they immediately split up—the two Nez Perce wolves going one way, the ten pups another. Unfortunately, the severe winter that year caused elk and deer reproduction to be a virtual bust, with much of the national park absent of its usual abundance of spring elk calves and deer fawns—the one type of prey these inexperienced wolves might have been able to kill. So they turned to livestock. Through 1997 fully two-thirds of all sheep and cattle killed by wolves could be traced to these Sawtooth pups; as a result, most were eventually removed by control actions. In the end only two of the animals remained, Numbers 70 and 72, sole survivors of an experiment gone bad.

◆ ◆ ◆

FOR ALL THE problems the Nez Perce wolves gave us, in at least one sense their release can be considered a success. The Yellowstone wolf plan had always called for reintroducing family groups—again, part of an effort to ease anxiety and discontent in the animals, thereby reducing their urge to wander. But the disintegration of the Nez Perce pack, whereby wolves left the acclimation pens and roamed alone, meant they eventually paired with other solitary wolves to form new packs. In the end Number 29 started the Gros Ventre Pack, while his siblings Number 26 and Number 30 began the Washakie and Thorofare packs, respectively. Including offspring from the original Nez Perce animals these wolves produced seven litters of pups—a significant contribution to the restoration of wolves in greater Yellowstone.

In nearly every other pack the use of acclimation pens seemed to reduce movements following release, and at the same time, helped maintain familial ties. In fact, so well did things go in these early stages that while the original reintroduction plan called for releases over three to five years, in the end we needed only two. (There was some debate over whether or not even a second year of reintroductions was necessary; we ended up going for it, primarily to increase genetic diversity.) We were truly "ahead of schedule and under budget," as the original wolf project leader Mike Phillips liked to say. And that was beautiful music to a lot of ears.

Portrait of a Wolf

NUMBER 10

Though his life was cut short in his prime, just weeks after walking out of the acclimation pen, Number 10 was arguably one of the most memorable wolves we've encountered. Outweighing nearly every other animal bound for Yellowstone, he was bolder, more confident than most—once again, markedly different from the very cautious Number 9. Veterinarian Mark Johnson recalls working with 10 at the holding facility near Hinton, Alberta. When it came time to administer a sedative, explains Johnson, which was accomplished by means of a syringe attached to the end of a long pole, the normal process was to try to distract an animal's attention away from the needle. Most times this was easy, with some of the more timid wolves being so uncomfortable they hid their faces in bales of straw. Not so with Number 10, who never looked away, never blinked. That sort of poise and self-assurance is something a lot of wolf researchers, myself included, have a great deal of respect for; so it was that long before he hit Yellowstone, 10 had for many in the wolf project already become a favorite.

Like so much of his too-short life, 10's walk out of the acclimation pen came with no lack of drama. The previous week we'd opened the pen gate to allow final release of the Crystal Creek wolves only to, as mentioned earlier, find them unwilling to leave. After much discussion, we decided to try to facilitate their movement out of the enclosure by cutting a hole elsewhere in the pen, in a place without such strong links to humans. We tested the idea on the Crystal Creek Pack, tossing a little incentive into the mix by way of a deer carcass placed just outside the freshly cut hole. Seventeen hours later, to our enormous relief, we picked up the signal from a motion detector placed near the opening, indicating the animals had at last departed. (We later discovered that either the wolves hadn't left the pen at all, meaning the equipment had misfired, or if they did, they'd come back. Eventually we figured out that the animals were leaving at night, only to slip back in again during the day. Whenever we checked they were in the pen, as if nothing was going on, but a quick scan of the area revealed tracks, some of which went straight to a winter-killed elk. Ultimately it would take the pack ten days to leave the pen for good.) Buoyed by our apparent success we decided to launch a similar cutting operation at the Rose Creek pen, as those wolves seemed to be having similar doubts about abandoning the enclosure. A team of us gathered at the Buffalo Ranch and began loading cutting tools, camera equipment, and a partial deer carcass onto a sled for the mile-long hike north to the pen site.

It was cold that day, a time of year not quite winter and not quite spring, the minutes and hours pushed by gusty winds and clouded by curtains of snow. Just south of the pen, at the lip of a small rise, we stopped for a moment to take stock of the situation. Surprisingly, Number 9 was pacing nervously back and forth. That was strange, because at the approach of humans this very cautious wolf would almost always take refuge in the rear of the pen, in her so-called comfort zone. As we stood there trying to figure out what was going on, suddenly there erupted the most soulful, yearning howl imaginable—not from inside the pen, but behind us, on an open hillside just to the east. We peered through the falling snow to see bold, magnificent Number 10 standing there, looking right at us. "Like a ghost," as one of the members described him. Clearly, this wolf had little of the reluctance to leave that others had displayed. More intriguing still was that he was hanging close by, waiting, possibly encouraging his newfound partner to take her own walk into the wilds. On one hand we were elated, very much caught up in the drama of the moment. But at the same time there was panic rising in our throats. What if our presence caused 10 to change his mind, abandon his mate to run off on his own across the frozen hills of Yellowstone? How fully bonded would two adults be who only ten weeks earlier were total strangers? Anxious to make tracks we abandoned our plan of cutting a hole in the back of the pen, dropped the deer carcass near the gate and then fumbled for a bit trying to figure out the least intrusive route out, finally choosing to hustle away down a sheltered ravine. All the while 10 was eying us, paralleling our route from a nearby ridge, howling. It was a startling, muscular show of authority, and it cut right through the bluster of that winter storm. We could hardly miss the message that seemed to be spilling out of his upturned muzzle: Number 10 wasn't just free. He was back in charge.

The end came for this beautiful wolf soon afterward, on a warm day in April east of Red Lodge, Montana, when a local man armed with a borrowed rifle dropped him with a single bullet. The shooter—testifying that he thought he was aiming at a wild dog—was later found guilty of the federal offense of killing an endangered species, sentenced to six months in jail and the loss of hunting and fishing privileges for two years. It was barely a month into the reintroduction, and already we'd lost one of the stars of the show. For me the entire incident was a bad dream come true. The critics were right, I remember thinking at the time—we just couldn't overcome hundreds of years of intense hatred toward wolves. To some people, as disturbing as the shooting itself was, more unsavory still was the reaction of a handful of locals who cheered the killing, calling it an act of heroism. A few suggested, and not entirely in jest, that it was just the sort of thing to make the guy an appealing candidate for governor.

For the rest of us, the memory of Number 10 lived on in his progeny—eight little wolves born to his mate, Number 9, laid down in a scrape of dirt under a Douglas-fir tree, on the northwest flank of Mount Maurice. He remains in many ways an ideal icon of this reintroduction: both a symbol of the extraordinary strength of wolves—their ability to thrive if given half a chance—and at the same time, a reminder of how frail such vitality can be in the face of humans who would wipe them from the earth.

CHAPTER 4
THE SHAPE OF
HOME

Getting a handle on why wolves do what they do has never been an easy proposition. Not only are there tremendous differences in both individual and pack personalities, but each displays a surprising range of behaviors depending on what's going on around them at any given time. No sooner will a young researcher think, "That's it, I've finally got a handle on how wolves respond in a particular situation," than they'll do something

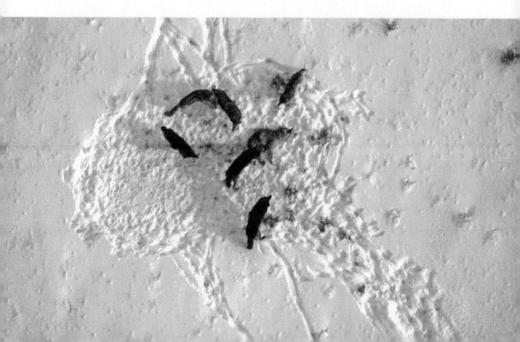

to prove him at least partially wrong. Those of us who've been in this business for very long have come to accept a professional life full of wrong turns and surprises. Clearly, this is an animal less likely to offer scientists irrefutable facts than to lure us on a long and crooked journey of constant learning.

Any discussion of how wolves establish and defend their territory needs to begin with the fact that not all packs in Yellowstone are created equal. The national park contains what might be best thought of as two distinct populations of wolves—one living on the northern range, the other occupying the interior. Wolves living in the northern system, at the heart of which is the Lamar Valley, enjoy a home turf generally lower in elevation than elsewhere in the park, where grass is more plentiful, and thermal features are few and far between. More elk winter here than in the entire rest of the park. Indeed the vast majority of the rest of the elk herds, except for a relatively small group known as the Madison-Firehole, will with the coming of snow and ice drift down and out of the national park altogether.[1] In most years a summering population of approximately 35,000 animals[2] has by December dropped to roughly 8,000, most of those concentrated on the northern range. This abundance of elk means an abundance of wolves—fully half the wolf population, living in less than a quarter of the national park. That situation provides us with a key to understanding behavior related to territory: specifically, wolf packs densely concentrated on the northern range means a high level of interpack conflict.

Meanwhile so-called "interior packs" have fewer prey resources. That forces them to supplant their winter diets with bison, and in at least one group—the Delta Pack—by moose. What's more, deeper snows in the interior of the park, along with the presence of thermal sites—warm, largely snow-free zones where prey animals gather to feed—have led to different hunting strategies. Here the wolves often take prey animals not merely by running them, as usually happens with the northern packs, but by trying to force them away from those warm zones into deep drifts of snow, where it's tougher to defend themselves.[3] Finally, and key to concerns about territory, is the fact that because there are fewer elk—their preferred prey—available in the interior of the park, the wolves there live in relatively isolated territories, making interpack skirmishes fairly rare. In short, so profoundly different are the conditions these two populations face, that the consequences of those differences show up in everything from the physical size of individual animals, to population growth, to the number of litters born to the packs. (On a side note, one of the great ongoing debates among wolf researchers is whether wolves kill more when prey is abundant, or if in fact they simply kill at a rate that keeps them minimally fed.[4] Our data in Yellowstone suggests the latter is true. Wolves on the northern range have five to six times as much prey available to them as interior packs, yet both groups kill at about the same rate. Not that wolves won't kill more if the prey is vulnerable, as we see every year in late winter, when elk are at their weakest. But at other times of year, taking down a healthy, well-fed ungulate is a dangerous business—so much so that wolves may only put themselves at risk when they're genuinely hungry.)

People often refer to all sorts of carnivores as being territorial—from cougars to bears, lynx to wolverines. But most of these use broadly overlapping home ranges, never defending them anywhere close to as vigorously as wolves do. Of all mammals, few can be considered territorial in the classic sense. But as we've seen time and again wolves definitely make the cut, ready at the drop of a hat to protect their home ground from other packs, sometimes ending up locked in ferocious battles that kill, maim, or otherwise injure the competition.

Because they ended up living closer to one another, the wolf packs released in and around the Lamar Valley during the first two years of the project would prove key to gaining new knowledge about territory. In March of 1995 we set free six members of the Crystal Creek wolf pack into the heart of the Lamar—again, one of three groups brought down from near Hinton, Alberta. The potential to make a good living here was hardly lost on Crystal Creek, whose members ended up wandering very little during that first year, finding everything they needed and then some right here. Likewise in that same spring would come the Rose Creek wolves. As previously noted, on walking free of the pen two members of this latter pack left the park to have pups, though the alpha male would die shortly before their birth in an illegal shooting. In an attempt to safeguard the new family we brought them back to the pen to allow the pups to mature. When the group was released again into the Lamar in the autumn of 1995 they drifted westward several miles, leaving the heart of the valley to Crystal Creek.

While both of these wolf packs enjoyed a fairly peaceful coexistence through the winter, things changed in a big way the following spring. It was then, in April of 1996 that we released another pack into the Lamar Valley near the base of Druid Peak. Given both the size of the area and the abundance of prey we assumed the Crystal Creek Pack— by then already firmly established in the Lamar—would bump these new wolves, known as the Druid Peak Pack, to the next best place without serious conflict. We were wrong. Considering the Druid Peak Pack came from a part of British Columbia with healthy wolf populations, in hindsight it makes good sense that they might arrive in Yellowstone with a highly protective, firmly territorial mindset, unconcerned whether or not there was excellent habitat with no competition not far from their release site. Besides, just as individual wolves show a wide range of personalities, so too do the packs themselves. And from the very beginning the Druids showed an exceptional fierceness—traveling widely, more than happy to take on any wolf they happened to run across. In other words, they had a territorial mentality with no territory.

The first major clash came just weeks after their release, in May of 1996, with the Crystal Creek wolves. The Crystal Creek Pack had denned in the east end of the Lamar valley that spring, in a loose patch of Douglas fir along Soda Butte Creek. No sooner did the Druids find them before they set about killing the alpha male, Number 4, and at the same time badly wounding his mate, alpha female Number 5. We're not sure, but it's quite likely they also killed the pups, which we looked for but never found. Shortly afterward Number 5 was seen in Lamar Valley, nursing her wounds; standing beside her was an unrelated two year-old male, Number 6, who by no small miracle appeared uninjured.

This violent encounter forced a new beginning for the Crystal Creek Pack. Together 5 and 6 started drifting south, arriving in twenty-five miles at what would be their home for many years, in the high, handsome Pelican Valley of central Yellowstone. (In time Number 5 and her mates would take a new name, Mollie's Pack, so designated in honor of Mollie Beattie, the courageous former director of the U.S. Fish and Wildlife Service, who died of a brain tumor shortly after the re-introduction. To pull off this project Mollie had held the line in the face of great antagonism. Following her death some of her ashes were sprinkled near the Crystal Creek pen.)

In all of North America, Pelican is one of the only valleys where you can find wolves, grizzlies, and bison. In a very real sense, what America was prior to European settlement this small basin in the middle of Yellowstone is yet today. Dan MacNulty, who's dedicated long hours to studying wolves and bison in Pelican, has said that if the Lamar is the heart of Yellowstone, as so many like to claim, then Pelican is the soul. During late spring and summer months the place is a Garden of Eden, giving rise to mile after mile of silver sage and Idaho fescue. True to its name, white pelicans can often be seen in the distance, drifting without a sound on motionless wings. As summer begins unfolding elk and bison pour in from the lower valleys, feasting on nutrient-rich grasses and forbs.

Yet for all its beauty and diversity, in winter this is arguably one of the harshest climates anywhere on the continent—a frigid weave of deep snow and bitter cold. Temperatures routinely bottom out at thirty or even forty below zero, with snows piling three and four feet deep. Elk, the preferred food of Yellowstone's wolves, are rarely found in that season—a shortage that each year forces Mollie's Pack to journey out to lower elevations. Yet, and for reasons we may never understand, they always return. On most winter days what survives here are a mere two hundred bison, many old and tough, super-sized behemoths that somehow manage to scrape out a bitter existence around the handful of thermal areas that remain free of snow. To save energy the bison move very little, thereby preserving their stored body fats. Even so, by the end of winter they're often weak, literally hanging on for dear life. Waiting for spring. And these days, watching for wolves.

For a wolf, even a weak bison can prove a phenomenally challenging foe. It would take Number 5 and the pack mates she eventually gathered around her several seasons to become bison hunters. But learn they did, driven by the same desperate circumstances as their prey. I remember watching film that Dan shot of two separate hunting events in 1999 involving Number 5 and thirteen other wolves, engaged in a battle with a single bull bison lasting just over nine hours. Again and again the wolves drove the bull into deep snow—a move meant to compromise his footing, his kicking power. That done, several members of the pack leapt onto his back, biting and tearing. Managing with great effort to free himself from the drifts, the bison then stopped and literally shook the wolves from his back, at the same time slashing with his head, trying his best to hook them with his horns. Over and over each animal pressed the other, both slowly wearing down. In most situations like this it would've been the wolves that gave in. Not this time. In the end the bison went down. The following year 5 would lead her pack in taking at least two more bison, though undoubtedly there were more, battling in what by then was a relatively old age with uncanny ferocity, never giving up. This, even though by that time her pack was down to a paltry four wolves.

Over the years the size of Mollie's Pack has stayed small. On only two occasions has it grown to more than ten animals, including once during the summer of 2003, when the pack swelled to twelve for a couple months, only to drop back down to seven by the following fall. Some think the pack might be of such modest size because of the high mortality associated with living off bison. Others wonder if it's the lack of suitable prey, which forces many of the pack members out in search of greener pastures—a notion our research with radio collars seems to corroborate.

While the group size may not be all that big, Mollie's wolves have consistently claimed some of the largest animals in the ecosystem. Out of the roughly three hundred wolf captures we've made in Yellowstone, only ten have pushed the scales over 130 pounds, and two of those animals came from Mollie's Pack. Incredibly, one winter we captured two male pups from the group weighing a whopping 120 pounds each— more than 30 pounds above average. While we can attribute some of that weight to meat in their stomachs (we caught them on a bison kill), still, they were among the largest pups found anywhere in the park. Both of these little giants have since left the pack, one disappearing west of Yellowstone, the other going on to become alpha male of the Slough Creek Pack. John Varley, a thirty-year veteran of Yellowstone, thinks such super-sizing may have to do with the fact that only larger wolves can survive those furious brawls with bison.

◆ ◆ ◆

As it turned out, the Druid wolves were just getting started. They kept traveling that summer, ever on the lookout to claim more territory. In June of 1996 they met the Rose Creek Pack in a place called Slough Creek, just west of the Lamar Valley. And though in this case the Rose Creek wolves held their own, it was merely a taste of what the Druids would be serving up in the seasons to come. For those watching nearby, it seemed like total bedlam: animals running everywhere, intermingling and then splitting off, leaving the human bystanders feeling like spectators at a sporting event for which both the rules of the game and the identity of the teams were lost in confusion. Those early days in general often found us standing around giddy as school kids, hardly able to believe what was going on right in front of our eyes. What's more, we were startled not only by what we saw happening between rival packs, but also between wolves and coyotes, grizzlies, moose, elk, and bison. Clearly, all this visibility provided some great learning opportunities. Yet at first, some of that learning was lost on us simply because our scientific protocols—those methods we depend on to decipher the meanings of such encounters—were just plain lacking.

I'd learned much about the craft of working with wolves from Rolf Peterson on Isle Royale, as well as in Minnesota with Dave Mech. Both men, having been pupils of famed wolf researcher Durward Allen, set up their studies around the use of aircraft. That approach had to do with the fact that in the North Woods you rarely see wolves at all unless you're flying over them, ideally in the winter months. In my own work at Isle Royale over nine summers and two winters I hiked, skied, and snowshoed some four thousand miles—this on an island of 210 square miles. During that entire period I spotted a wolf from the ground only three times. Absent any good chance to sight the animals, as researchers we instead grew adept at examining sign, knowing when things were "red hot," which meant finding tracks or feces just a few hours old. We examined prey animals killed by wolves, not to mention dissected every scat we found. The project changed in 1988 with the coming of radio collars (though to this day Rolf Peterson wonders if we really know that much more than we did when we were just out there hiking our legs off). Meanwhile over in Minnesota, in a study focusing on more wolf packs over a much larger area, radio tracking had been used from the very beginning. Supervised by Dave Mech, the project was based on capturing, collaring, and then tracking on a regular basis.

When it came to devising a research model for Yellowstone, we ended up drawing on this work at Isle Royale and in Minnesota—especially when it came to collecting data with radio collars. This kind of approach makes especially good sense when you consider the size of Yellowstone—some two million acres. Each of the forty-one wolves introduced to the park in 1995 through 1997 (this number includes the infamous Sawtooth pups) were outfitted with transmitting devices. But again, there was no protocol in our toolbox for how to watch wolves on the ground with our own eyes. At first I simply told field crews to take good notes, but in no time at all that left us drowning in paperwork. Desperate to come up with a more efficient means of gathering information, we eventually developed some of the most complex observational data forms imaginable. These address specific questions about interactions between wolves and between wolves and their prey, as well as leadership behavior, encounters with non-prey animals, and so on. "We're constantly revamping our forms," notes our data manager Deb Guernsey, "because we're always thinking of new questions."

All things being equal, securing more territory means having a better shot at finding food. But whether or not as a wolf you can actually pull down more real estate, or for that matter, even protect what you already have, depends on several factors. For starters having a big pack can help, allowing you to basically throw your weight around when and where you see fit. In fact, we now suspect that forming a pack on the hotly contested ground of the northern range isn't even possible for a mere pair of wolves—at least those who've tried it so far have failed.[5] By all indications, in this competitive environment at least three or more wolves are necessary to hold turf against larger packs. Beyond pack numbers, the age of individual animals is also important; in the world of wolves, experience counts for an awful lot. Even the size of the wolves can be a factor.

Still another consideration has to do with whether the fight takes place on your territory or someone else's—what might be called "home field advantage." It's a lot easier in your own backyard, after all, to know the best escape routes, even where to cross a swollen river. Way back when, during that crazy fracas in June of 1996, the Rose Creek wolves had this kind of advantage, and the Druids didn't. At least in part because of that, despite the Druid wolves having picked the fight, Rose Creek quickly took the upper hand. As wolves are known to do in the face of such battles, Rose Creek wasted no time targeting Druid's lead pair—the alpha male and female. In a stunning piece of drama the alpha female, Number 39, was chased at full tilt into the swollen flood waters of Slough Creek. Suddenly, she was swimming for her life. Unable to stay long in the raging currents, she spotted a fallen tree lying in the water a short distance downstream and began swimming like mad in a mighty effort to reach it. She made it, too, struggling up and onto the trunk, looking like nothing so much as a miserable, waterlogged cat.

Amazingly, during this particular fight not a single wolf was killed. It was rather the aftermath of the battle that proved deadly. Three days later Roger Stradley and I were flying in the Super Cub when a couple miles from the site of the skirmish we found a dead Rose Creek wolf— a yearling male, Number 20, lying just up the steep bank of Buffalo Fork Creek. My best guess is that the excitement of the encounter had drawn the young Rose Creek wolf into chasing the fleeing Druids; drawn away from the safety of his pack mates the rebuffed Druids turned on him, making easy work of their lone aggressor.

The unlucky Number 20, by the way, became the first wolf casualty in Yellowstone to be picked up by means of a pack mule. This sort of recovery reflects a longstanding management policy of Yellowstone, where with few exceptions, we travel the backcountry by traditional means. That means by foot or horseback summer to fall, and in winter, by skis or snowshoes. Which is just fine with me. Having grown up riding horses (and in truth, having for years felt overrun by the motors of the world), I'm well aware that pack stock isn't just easier on the land than vehicles are, but they're also simpler to maneuver on tough terrain. The bottom line is that a truck has yet to be invented that could pull up alongside a dead wolf on the rock-strewn hillside of Buffalo Fork Creek, with several knee-deep swamps barring the approach.

Again, playing a key role in wolf operations from the beginning—managing not only these sorts of recoveries, but regular feeding operations when wolves were in the acclimation pens—have been top-notch horse and mule packers. One of them is a fourth-generation Montanan by the name of Ben Cunningham, the man who pulled the mule up to Number 20 that day. This was a delicate maneuver—not just due to the sharp terrain, but also because the scent of a wolf is not something most stock animals react to calmly. Slowly, carefully, the wolf's lifeless body was lifted and secured to the top of the mule—the poor mule's eyes bulging with nervous energy—at which point we turned him and headed back the ten miles to the trailhead. It all went beautifully. After work we sidled up to a table in the K-Bar in Gardiner, Montana, until nearly 10 P.M., talking on about the first wolf ever pulled out of the Yellowstone backcountry the old cowboy way. I made a decision right then and there: Ben was going to have to come along every time there was similar work to be done.

Years later, as the winter of 2000–2001 unfolded, the Druids moved west through the Lamar Valley, drifting still again into Rose Creek territory. By this point Rose Creek was no small pack—sixteen strong, after an earlier population peak of twenty-four. But then again, it was a motley group. Though two litters of pups had been born in 2000 the pack was never really united, circulating through their territory in disjointed fashion. Not a good thing when the Druids come to call. During a tracking flight on November 23, 2000, I was lucky enough to witness a spirited encounter between the two packs on Slough Creek flats—ground that Rose Creek had claimed since the earliest days of the reintroduction. For the Druids, moving about with twenty-seven wolves made for cumbersome traveling, with some animals always lagging behind; on this particular day, only six pack members were on the scene. From what we could tell sitting overhead in the airplane, Druid sensed the presence of other wolves while still a couple of miles away. Not having seen the Rose Creek animals ourselves, but rather taking our cues from the Druids' sudden, hurried movement, we started looking, listening for radio signals. Sure enough, pretty soon we laid eyes on a ragtag group of Rose Creek wolves—two pups, with one lone adult female calling the shots.

Once Druid Peak actually sighted the Rose Creek wolves, the two Druid alphas, 42 and 21, wasted no time running straight at them. While the Rose Creek youngsters seemed hesitant, lost in confusion, there was no such uncertainty in the adult, female Number 155. In the blink of an eye she was off and running for her life. At this point the Druid Pack split apart, before long catching the two Rose Creek pups. After slipping on the ice and getting several bites, one fortunate youngster was given a reprieve when commotion elsewhere drew her attackers away. A short time later another pup was caught and pinned down, and from what we could see from the tracking plane he was a sure casualty. A minute or so later his attackers caught sight and sound of the Rose Creek adult escaping down Slough Creek and took off in hot pursuit. When the dust settled we flew back to pinpoint the carcass of that ill-fated pup, wanting to memorize the location in order to retrieve the carcass. When we couldn't find it I radioed the ground crew, who'd also watched the attack, asking if they knew where he was. I could hardly believe my ears. The pup had run off!

This little wolf may have gained deliverance in part because he was young, and therefore not inclined to fight back. Besides being fright-

ened, a wolf would at this stage of his life be accustomed to low ranking status in his pack. It would be nothing new for him, in the face of
angry adults, to simply give up—an act of surrender that may have reduced the enthusiasm of his attackers. That, combined with the chaos
of other wolves running around nearby, may explain how this lucky
pup stumbled away to live another day.

From then on the Rose Creek wolves continued to lose more and
more territory to the Druids. Even so, we wondered if such gains would
be enough to maintain a megapack of twenty-seven animals. (The
number of the Druid wolves would later grow higher still, to thirty-
seven.) Beside the basic issue of finding enough food, it's hard to imagine that in such a large pack social dynamics wouldn't be strained. We
rarely saw all the wolves together as a single unit, the animals preferring instead to live and travel in several groups. In time there would
come an actual splitting apart of the Druids, each faction taking in
dispersing wolves from other nearby packs, forming elements of the
Slough Creek, Geode Creek, Buffalo Fork, and Agate Creek packs.
Meanwhile the alpha male and female, numbers 21 and 42, carried on,
still anchoring what had been traditional Druid territory.

Interpack skirmishes have been increasing on the northern range for
some time now—a situation almost sure to lead to additional wolf
mortality. Curiously, several long-term studies elsewhere in North
America suggest these conflicts are prompted by a lack of prey.[6] As elk
numbers decline wolves get hungry, which draws them into new country in search of food, which inevitably results in their trespassing on another pack's territory. With trespass come fights, and with fights, often
death. This is one reason some scientists—including early on Douglas
Pimlott, a pioneer Canadian wolf researcher working in Algonquin
Park, Ontario, as well as Adolph Murie—have thought of wolf populations as being "self regulatory,"[7] their numbers controlled in part simply through the elimination of rivals. Despite this idea being nearly

universally rejected,[8] right now we're seeing a stabilization of wolf numbers on Yellowstone's northern range even though prey isn't lacking. Though it's hard for us to say for sure, perhaps even with plenty of food on hand, wolf territories can only be compressed so much before deadly conflicts begin to erupt.

The northern range, with its rich resources, was quickly becoming center stage for an incredible amount of action and intrigue. And there was lots more wolf drama still to come.

Portrait of a Wolf

NUMBER 42

THE SHEER SIZE of the Druid Peak Pack in 2001—along with the fact they often lived, right out in front of us, what seemed like epic lives, full of struggle and conquest—made for some of the most unforgettable encounters of the past ten years. To those who saw them from the national park's northeast entrance road before the break-up, sometimes twenty or more animals cruising through the Lamar Valley like they were the best and brightest game in town, it will no doubt remain one of the great wolf watching experiences of all time. Literally thousands of people saw this pack in their heyday; indeed, it's probably safe to say that the Druid Peak animals became the most frequently viewed wolf pack in the world.

An early matriarch of the Druid Peak Pack was the exceptionally forceful, no-nonsense female Number 40, who in 1996 seemed to wrest control of the group from her mother, Number 39. Shortly after this apparent coup mom left the pack to wander on her own for nearly a year, later returning to the group—possibly drawn back by a nearly irresistible urge to help rear pups born in the spring of 1997. Number 40 tolerated her presence, but barely. In late summer of 1997, 39 left again to travel alone until December, when she wandered eastward out of the park. Sadly, someone awakened by a dog barking in the middle of the night shined a light into the darkness and ended up shooting what he thought was a coyote, killing Number 39.

From 1997 to 2000, then, Number 40 was the undisputed leader— some might say full-blown tyrant—of the Druid Peak wolves. No one challenged her. By all indications one had only to look cross-eyed at this alpha to find herself slammed to the ground with a bared set of canines poised above her neck. Few wolves have been as frequently observed as Number 40, and she was never shy about showing off her personality. Throughout her life she was fiercely committed to always having the upper hand, far more so than any other wolf we've observed in Yellowstone. The family member receiving the brunt of her punishment was her sister, Number 42—an animal whose long suffering at the hands of her cruel sister would be portrayed in two National Geographic films, leading the creators of those programs to dub her the Cinderella wolf.

In 1999 Number 42 split off from the main pack and began digging a den not far from the group's traditional den site, which at the time was being used by Number 40. Not long after 42 finished the job she received a visit from her foul-tempered sister, who wasted no time handing down one of the nasty trouncings she'd become famous for. As had happened countless times before, 42 did nothing to fight back—simply laid there and took it. Never again was she seen near her freshly excavated den. Given that wolves only dig dens for the purpose of giving birth, those of us watching were intensely curious about whether 42 had in fact had pups. Still, because we try never to disturb wolves during the denning period, afraid that our presence might have negative effects, all we could do is sit back, wait, and wonder. Finally, when it became obvious that the den was completely abandoned we shouldered our day packs and hiked in to check it out. There was no evidence of pups, though by then it had been long enough that another animal could have easily stumbled upon the site and devoured them. Whether Number 42 actually gave birth or simply experienced a "pseudo-pregnancy"—essentially a false pregnancy, which causes a female to behave like she's pregnant—we'll never know.

The next year, though—in 2000—things went rather differently, providing another first for those of us in the business of studying wild wolves. As mentioned earlier, in that year three females of the Druid Peak Pack dug dens and all three had pups. Number 40, the alpha female, used the pack's traditional den. Meanwhile Number 106, a low-ranking wolf in the pack, excavated a site several miles away, at Pebble Creek. Finally there was Number 42, who went the other direction, this time digging her den in a loose cluster of trees in the middle of the Lamar Valley. Wolf motherhood brings with it a nearly constant demand for nursing, which means in the time immediately following birth the females rarely get a chance to leave the den. For this reason it's extremely helpful to have other adults around to lend a hand. Few of those other adults visited the foul-tempered Number 40 at the main den site, leaving her to rely mostly on her mate—that fine alpha male, a wolf long on patience, Number 21. Due to her low social ranking there was even less help around for 106, who remained mostly alone.

Number 42, however, the so-called Cinderella wolf, was routinely assisted by numerous adult females, most notably two sisters born into the pack three years earlier, numbers 103 and 105.

Life at a wolf den is for the most part calm and peaceful. Alpha females typically pick secluded places that offer both shade and water, though on a few occasions I've seen dens excavated out in the open sun. Pups poke their heads out roughly ten to fourteen days after birth, stumbling into the world totally reliant on the pack, and especially their mother, until they're about two months old. As small and clumsy as they are at first, the pups mature rapidly. Needle sharp teeth come in fast, leading their mothers to begin weaning at about five weeks. I've watched nursing wolves around this time, burdened by five or more little pups scurrying to their teats for another meal, and I could almost see the females wince in pain. Needless to say, as the weeks go by the bouts of nursing get shorter and shorter, finally stopping altogether, at which point the pups begin to consume solid meat.

Six weeks after the pups were born, Number 42 and her faithful cadre of female attendants decided to head out for a jaunt. Near Number 40's den site the troupe stumbled across the old matriarch herself, and as usual, she lit into Number 42 with what even for her was tremendous ferocity. Then, as if wanting to make up for recent lost opportunities she turned on Number 105, determined to give her a good thrashing as well. Soon thereafter all the wolves, including Number 40, headed back in the direction of Number 42's den site. By this time it was growing dark, leaving those of us watching in the lurch, desperate to know what would happen next.[1] That a lot did happen that night, though, there can be no doubt. The next morning Number 40 showed up in the Lamar Valley near the Buffalo Ranch, about a mile from Number 42's den site—bloody and staggering, barely able to stand.

Among the first on the scene was biologist Kerry Murphy— "Murph," as we like to call him. Number 40 was in such bad shape, her

wounds so severe, Murph thought she'd surely been hit by a car, perhaps trapped under the carriage and knocked against the pavement. He
couldn't imagine other wolves inflicting such damage. I got the call just
as we were about to take off from the Gardiner Airport on a routine
tracking flight; still not sure what had really happened, continuing to
think 40 had been hit by a car, we decided to bring her in and tend her
wounds. (Only when animals are hurt by humans—an "unnatural
event," in other words, such as being hit by a car—is it considered ap-
propriate to intervene. Had we known Number 40 was attacked by
other wolves we would've simply let nature take its course.) As it turned
out, despite having made the decision to help we never got the chance.
Moving to place 40 in the back of a pickup truck, Murph simply
walked over and picked her up—an unheard of act when it comes to
wild wolves. Within minutes of loading her for transport, this feisty,
aggressive matriarch of the Druid Pack—the wolf avoided by most and
feared by all—was dead. Of course we'll never know exactly what happened. But assembling available clues, we imagined events unfolding
something like this:

Shortly after dark a massive fight broke out, somewhere near Number 42's den site. Unlike the clash in 1999, though, this time 42 had no
intention of letting the testy alpha get anywhere near her pups. We
assume that as the wolves drew near to 42's den, with 40 close behind,
42 turned and attacked her sister. Much as happens with dogs, when a
fight breaks out among two wolves other members are quickly re-
cruited into the skirmish, each taking the side of her ally. For Number
40, allies were in short supply. It was payback time. We know from
checking radio collar signals that besides Number 42, at least two other
adult wolves were probably involved in the attack, including the two
sisters, 103 and 105. Besides leaving Number 40 with a ruptured jugu-
lar artery, later determined to be the actual cause of death, her carcass
was riddled with enough holes and cuts to suggest an attack of horrific

proportions. One wound on the back of her neck was so deep I could bury my index finger all the way to the knuckle with room left over.

If our version of the story is correct, it represents the first time in the scientific record that an alpha wolf has been killed by her own sub-ordinates.[2] Admittedly, it's not impossible that Number 40 was killed by another wolf pack. Yet the battle occurred in the middle of Druid Peak territory, whereas the vast majority of territorial skirmishes with other packs happen near the edges. Furthermore, we know from radio collar signals that at the time of the fight none of the wolves from neighboring packs were anywhere close to the middle of the Lamar Valley.

For the remaining members of Druid Peak life went on without skipping a beat. Over the next four to six days Number 42 was seen carrying her pups one by one in her mouth to the traditional Druid Peak den, a site that recently had been fully and fiercely under the control of Number 40. Even more intriguing is the fact that not only did Number 42 end up adopting and raising the former alpha female's pups right alongside her own, but she also welcomed in low-ranking Number 106 and her offspring. And so it was that in the summer of 2000 three separate litters of pups—twenty-one animals in all—were raised in a single den. Clearly the tyrant was out, and in her place had come a far more benevolent leader. (Wolf project employee Rick McIntyre has wondered if simply being out from under the force of Number 40 allowed some of the lower ranking Druid females to finally come into their own. Despite her low status, for example, Number 106 would after 40's death show herself to be highly capable of leadership, becoming among other things the finest hunter in the pack. Today she remains a tireless and, by all appearances, benevolent leader of the Geode Creek Pack.)

On the last day of January, 2004, Number 42 was involved in what we believe was a clash with Mollie's Pack. It would be her last. While both circumstantial evidence and a careful necropsy confirmed that her death was indeed due to wolves, we're not entirely sure which ones, since there were two rival packs in the area. Miraculously her mate— Number 21, formerly a partner to the ill-tempered 40—escaped unscathed, even though this particular rumble happened during breeding season, when the two were almost never more than a few feet apart. If it was in fact Mollie's Pack that delivered the fatal blow the tale becomes one Shakespeare would love—the queen wolf dead, an act of revenge after all those years following the eviction of Mollie's Pack (then called the Crystal Creek wolves) from the Lamar Valley. Of course wolves aren't wired that way. Number 42 died along the pack's territorial boundary, where on any given day there exists a high danger of being fatally wounded in a skirmish.

At the time of 42's death the Druid Peak Pack was bigger than Mollie's, seventeen animals versus seven. That might lead one to think the outcome of the fight would be a foregone conclusion—especially since Mollie's Pack were the invaders, not in possession of "home field advantage." But of Druid's seventeen wolves nine were pups—animals without a lick of experience to draw on, sure to be less than helpful when things got ugly. In contrast Mollie's Pack had only two pups, which for all practical purposes made the fight between eight and five. Furthermore, we believe the Druid pack was split. An uncollared female nicknamed "U-black"—so called because of a U-shaped marking on her chest fur—along with another female wanderer, Number 255, were likely out soliciting males (behavior not much seen before Yellowstone), making the numbers more or less equal. Remember too that 21 and 42 of the Druids were by then old-timers, both about eight years old, and not as big as Mollie's wolves.

The other group nearby was the Agate Creek Pack, and indeed 42 died fairly close to their den site. We ultimately pinned her death on Mollie's wolves, though, in part because it correlated perfectly with one of the rare trips this pack made to Druid Peak territory. What's more, having territory immediately adjacent to the Druids had given the Agate Creek wolves a certain familiarity (some of the Agate wolves are in fact old Druid wolves). In the past the two groups had sometimes come within view of each other while skirting the common edge of the two territories, yet nothing happened. Given such an uneasy truce, why would they on this particular day decide to attack? And finally, at the time of 42's death the Agate Creek Pack had even less firepower than did Mollie's, sporting only three adults.

Given her gentle personality, along with distinct markings that made her easy to recognize, 42 had become a fast favorite to the crowds of wolf watchers routinely gathered along the national park's northeast entrance road. Following news of her death my e-mail was flooded, the phone ringing off the hook. Those who'd followed the story of the Yellowstone wolves truly lamented this animal's passing, as did many of us working for the wolf project. After visiting her body atop Specimen Ridge I discussed the experience with several people waiting beside the road for news, some of whom broke down in tears.

The death of 42 ended the opening chapter of wolf reintroduction in Yellowstone. She'd been one of the original animals to come to the national park in 1996 from British Columbia—what we often called a founder wolf. With her passing, none of the animals reintroduced from Canada remained.

CHAPTER 5
FILLING THE WILDS
WITH WOLVES

During the initial years of the Yellowstone wolf reintro-duction, while we were actively bringing in animals, the annual growth rate of the national park wolf population was roughly 40 to 50 percent. More than a few people heard those stats, did some fast figuring in their heads and ran off to tell the world the sky was falling, that wolves would soon overtake us all. But such rates are similar to other places where wolf numbers have

been severely clipped, often by 80 to 90 percent, through the use of government-sponsored control programs. (The major difference is that while wolf populations in other areas grew not just from reproduction, but from wolves moving in from surroundings areas, Yellowstone had no would-be immigrants nearby. Here all the growth was based on reproduction.) Like a great many other animals, from beavers to coyotes, wolves tend to expand fastest when their numbers are well below the carrying capacity of the ecosystem. In simplest terms, animals able to react to new opportunities in their environment—in this case, enjoying plentiful food resources and relatively few competitors—often exhibit a rapid increase in number. For a time wolf survival was high enough, about 80 percent for all age and sex classes, and mortality low enough that the population grew every year, settling in after the reintroduction phase to about 10 percent annually. The exceptions were 1998–1999, when we think a disease called parvovirus may have hit the pups, as well as in 2004–2005, which may prove to be the point when the wolf population actually started leveling off.

The Yellowstone landscape those first animals stumbled into back in 1995 was surely the wolf version of paradise. In most areas where wolves live, after all, dispersing animals of breeding age leave their home territory only to encounter a world filled with other wolf packs—each one entrenched, not inclined to welcome strangers. Vacancies can be tough to come by, and more than a few end up being killed for trespassing where they don't belong. In the early years at Yellowstone, though, adolescent animals had only to move next door to existing packs to find lands blissfully free of competition.

In order to put the movement and growth of Yellowstone's wolf population into better perspective, it may help to note that here, as elsewhere, are found two different kinds of packs. The first, referred to as "simple," is comprised of a breeding pair along with pups. Complex packs, meanwhile, in addition to the current year's pups also contain animals born in previous years—in Yellowstone, perhaps even four or five years before—thereby creating a multi-generational group. Whether a pack is simple or complex is the primary driving force behind how the group manages on a day-to-day basis. With simple packs, the fact that pups lack any basic skills for determining where to go, what prey to take, or even how to take it (not to mention their lousy fighting ability), means the alphas take care of just about everything. In complex packs, on the other hand, besides the pups there are always other "experts" around willing and able to help.

Most wolves in Yellowstone live in complex packs. In much of the rest of North America the opposite is true, likely because of human exploitation.[1] In most of these other places, after all, wolves are hunted, often intensively, which leads to a constant breaking up of the family. New packs are always forming, and that keeps the structure simple. Thanks to protections offered here in Yellowstone, though, seventeen of the nineteen wolf packs that have formed since 1995 are still around. Though this is still a speculative idea, such security may allow a kind of a cultural inertia to settle in, whereby once a pack is formed it tends to stay in place by means of adults passing down their experiences to younger generations. True, hard times may cause the number of wolves in the group to dwindle. But a remnant pack will usually continue to survive, rebounding when conditions improve. In addition, world renowned wolf researcher Rolf Peterson believes complex packs are also more common when the main prey is large, like moose or bison. The bigger and tougher the prey, his thinking goes, the more experience the pack needs to pull off a kill.

The story of a growing Yellowstone wolf population would prove to be about much more than young wolves simply hooking up with partners and breeding. Some of the greatest scientific findings of this project have come from watching how these animals made hay from an empty countryside overflowing with prey, often employing strategies that ended up shredding what we'd long thought of as so-called "normal" behaviors. For starters, for the first time in history we recorded pups only ten months old breeding in the wild. When female pup Number 16 was this age, for example, she ended up breeding with her stepfather, Number 8; several years later the shoe was on the other foot, when 16 bred with male pup Number 165 of the Leopold Pack.

But that was just the beginning. More often than not wolf packs have only one litter of pups each year—the offspring of the alpha male and female.[2] (In this book, by the way, we still use "alpha" to describe the breeding pair, though in the scientific community that term is falling out of fashion.) Yet starting in 1996 and continuing to this day, at least one pack in the park has had more than one litter per season; indeed, in some years there's been a group having three litters. By their nature wolves tend to avoid inbreeding—a fact vividly portrayed in the winter of 2002–2003, when the alpha male of the Druid Peak Pack tried to breed with his daughter, over the course of a single day making more than a half-dozen attempts to mount her, only to be met with a good hundred or so nips by the female. The following day this young female wandered away from her pack and almost immediately found a lone male nearby, one with whom she'd already bred a few days earlier—a Casanova wolf of sorts, who'd made something of an art out of slinking through other pack's territories without getting caught. Afterward she returned to her natal pack.[3]

Though not exactly common, this is the more typical way multiple litters happened in Yellowstone—a non-alpha female leaving the family for a short time to breed with males from other packs. Several times we've actually seen temporary clusters of ten or twelve wolves coming together to check each other out, some of which go on to breed with multiple partners. One February a wolf from the park's interior traveled all the way to the northern range to join one of these gatherings, where he bred with a couple different females before returning to his home turf near Old Faithful. All that's required for such trysts are females look-ing for the opportunity, along with non-territorial males willing to risk trespassing in order to find partners in somebody else's backyard. It's been especially fascinating to discover that by all appearances females seem tolerant of these wandering males not just during breeding season, but in other times of the year, as well. We've seen such travelers show-ing up at both den and rendezvous sites and be perfectly accepted—at least as long as none of the males of the pack are around. Should one of those males return, though, the intruder will waste no time packing it in and bolting away.[4]

Once a young female is impregnated she may return to her own group, only to move off alone when she's about to give birth to find a den site of her own. Later, when the pups are slightly older, she may either bring them back to the pack's main den and raise them there, or alternatively, try to tough it out alone through the summer. Wolf 103 is a good example of this latter behavior, having raised three pups alone with little help from other pack members—a decision that caused her no end of headaches, sometimes struggling even to fend off attacks by lowly coyotes.

More exceptional still in Yellowstone are cases where an alpha male breeds with other females in his pack not related by blood. We may have actually contributed to this sort of behavior by placing unrelated animals together in the acclimation pens. In such cases the alpha male, if so moved, could breed with several females, which is exactly what we saw happening in the Rose Creek, Chief Joseph, and Druid packs. (Alpha females, by the way, have never been seen breeding with any-one but the alpha male.) All this said, it's important to understand that by and large alpha pairs are monogamous. Even in those unusual cases where the alpha male ends up breeding with an animal other than the alpha female, his "pair bond" as scientists call it—the animal he tends to, is fiercely steadfast toward—remains always the alpha female. (A very good way to tell which wolves in a group are the alpha pair, though not entirely fool-proof, is to watch for behavior called double scent marking. This involves one of the pair urinating, and then the other urinating in the exact same spot.) Should a mate die, though, and the surviving alpha maintains her position in the pack, she'll readily take up with another wolf. Typically these new mates come from outside the pack, just as Number 21 of the Rose Creek Pack did in December of 1997, sensing the sudden vacancy in the Druids and moving right in. Likewise female Number 9 of Rose Creek had at least three mates in her life. This sometimes leads to situations where the breeding pair are of different ages.

This fierce loyalty between alpha pairs reflects the fact that wolves evolved to be highly dependent on solid family units, or packs. These families, perhaps not unlike our own, benefit greatly from strong, consistent leadership—by being able to follow a male and female that, besides being strong and healthy, have an essential ability to make sound decisions about everything from hunting to defending territory.

The frequency with which multiple litters have occurred in Yellowstone—perhaps 10 percent of all births have come about this way—may have something to do with the high population density of wolves on the northern range. In this part of the park there's simply more opportunity for it to happen, and so now and then it does—at least so long as prey is abundant. As mentioned earlier, in the year 2000 three females in the Druid Peak Pack produced twenty-one pups, twenty of which survived—catapulting the pack size to an amazing thirty-seven wolves, quite possibly the largest ever recorded. The only potentially bigger wolf pack was noted by wolf researcher Lu Carbyn in Wood Buffalo National Park in Alberta, Canada, when he spotted forty-two wolves together. In that region, though, in certain seasons wolves often follow migrating bison, collapsing their normal territoriality. Whether the group of wolves Lu saw was actually one pack or a mix of several is hard to say.

Multiple litters have been recorded elsewhere, including Alaska and the Northwest Territories, yet in these other places too it seems definitely more the exception than the rule.[5] Even when packs do have two or three litters, the survival of the second or third generally tends to be so poor that by fall the total number of pups is about what it would've been with only a single litter. Even in Yellowstone, out of approximately eighteen cases of wolf packs having more than one litter, we've recorded only one high-survivor event like the one we saw with Druid Peak in the year 2000—once again, a level of success that may be thanks to the abundant food supply. Indeed, between elk, bison, mule deer, and an occasional moose, the wolves of Yellowstone's northern range probably have the highest known biomass of prey available anywhere in the world.[6]

When it comes to breeding behavior, these somewhat remarkable games of musical chairs have left us with a lot of unanswered questions. To learn more we've been leaning on not just direct observation and radio collars, but also genetic techniques like DNA fingerprinting. Using blood taken during collaring operations, these genetic profiles allow us to not only study multiple females in the same pack, but basically genotype all the wolves we capture to see who their parents and other relatives are. In cases where we're not able to actually catch a key wolf, but manage to see the spot where it defecates, we can collect feces and then genotype it using stray cells from the intestine. Right now we're hunting for just such a sample from the new uncollared alpha male of the Druid pack, nicknamed "New Black." This work is being conducted at Robert Wayne's world-renowned lab at the University of California, Los Angeles.

Beyond all our current theories and speculations, there's an enormous wild card that gets played out time and again in wolf society, and it has to do with personalities. Wolf Number 40 ruled the Druid Peak Pack with an iron fist, always the one in charge, while Number 7, alpha female of the Leopold Pack, seemed to manage her group by applying what was a far more gentle nature. Such character differences probably also determine which one of the alphas, male or female, ends up being the primary leader of the group. In the case of 40, she routinely initiated activity and generally led the group more often than did her mate. The personality card influences much of what wolves do and how they do it—from their willingness to suffer captivity, to the level of playfulness they exhibit, to whether or not they leave their natal pack to seek a life elsewhere. All in all wolves display a fantastic degree of individuality, which in turn makes nearly every theory we come up subject to frequent and sudden second thoughts.

Number 5, left

Portrait of a Wolf

NUMBER 5

SUMMER OF 2000. Veteran radio tracking pilot Roger Stradley and I are hanging in the sky some five hundred feet above the wilds of central Yellowstone, drifting over a ghostly sweep of charred tree trunks from the 1988 fires. It's July, the season when wolves move their pups to rendezvous sites, when elk and their young are climbing across grassy swales and through broken forests, heading for higher elevations. In the past five years Roger and I have spent a good thousand hours together in this tiny Piper Super Cub, scanning the ground first in 1995 for three wolf packs, then six packs by 1997, and by 2005, fifteen. This time is different. Today we're looking hard for one wolf in particular—a kind of celebrity of the reintroduction, a matriarch who spent five years as alpha female of the Crystal Creek Pack. Number 5 was the very first wolf to actually arrive in Yellowstone in 1995, huddled in a metal crate and carried into an acclimation pen with the whole world watching, surrounded by Secretary of Interior Bruce Babbitt, the late director of the Fish and Wildlife Service Mollie Beattie, wolf project director Mike Phillips, and then-superintendent of Yellowstone, Michael Finley. There she'd spend the next ten weeks, walking to freedom in the third week of March. On the last couple tracking flights we haven't been able to find her. We're determined to uncover what happened.

Wolf Number 5, along with females 9 and 14, were in many ways the centerpiece of Yellowstone wolf recovery. They were the original alpha females, the lead animals of the wolf world—responsible not just for denning and giving birth, but also for making daily decisions about establishing territory and hunting for food. But for Number 5, life hadn't been easy. One year after leaving the acclimation pen she gave birth to a litter of pups, all of which were likely killed in a fight with those ruffians of greater Yellowstone, the Druid Peak Pack—a brawl that also brought the death of her mate, Number 4. Her pack all but destroyed, she herself severely injured, 5 hobbled out of the Lamar Valley with a single young male in tow, moving south toward the lush grasslands of the Pelican Valley. With this move, though it was made under difficult circumstances, she would take the steps that would later allow her to establish the first pack in central Yellowstone; that, in turn, provided a springboard for other packs to begin forming in this part of the park. She and the other wolves that in time gathered around her would become among the first of the bison hunters—chased and kicked and generally sent packing by the bison time and again, until at last they got it right.

Through years of weekly tracking flights we'd managed to locate Number 5 nearly every time: watching as she led pack mates along the edges of the lodgepole forest in search of elk, going head-to-head with moose on the banks of Pelican Creek, or even tangling—sometimes for hours at a time—with the nearly invincible bison. Yet as of late she'd been showing her age, looking ever more gray. There'd also appeared a black line under one eye, ever more pronounced, almost like the bags a person might get from not sleeping enough. Over the past winter we noticed her sometimes lagging behind her pack mates, struggling through the deep snow. We last made visual contact with her in January of the preceding winter, on her home ground in the Pelican Valley. As we flew over she looked up at us, just as she had so many times before. But this time it was a different look. Her eyes seemed changed, as if something had gone out of them. Where her gaze before seemed defiant, almost like she was daring us to try something, suddenly she seemed worried at our approach, as though the plane might do something terrible to her.

Finding her proves fairly easy. I spot her lying on her side on the ground below, her beautiful, ivory-colored coat looking stark against the black husk of a burned log. As we circle I notice she looks big, full in body—a good sign that at least she hasn't starved. We keep turning and turning, trying to get her to move, watching for a lift of the head, a twitch of a leg. While steady circling in the plane almost always produces some sort movement in a wolf, we get nothing. I make a mental note of the spot, but on our next overflight a week later, she's gone. We continue to search actively for weeks, then more sporadically for months after that. Years later I'll catch myself scanning for her radio collar frequency, hoping to hear that comforting beep indicating a live animal. A few times I'll even think I hear it, but sadly these turn out to be "ghost" beeps—a common occurrence when one radio tracks so much, spending thousands of hours listening to static through head-phones. One time I'll tell Roger about it, ask him to listen, but he won't be able to pick it up. Not that he'll come out and tell me that, mind you—just simply fail to acknowledge it. Out of respect, I suppose, knowing all too well how much I want to hear it.

CHAPTER 6

THE COMING OF THE
WOLF WATCHERS

Most days it begins before dawn. Cars creep through the murky light, rolling in from Cooke City or Silver Gate, or from the opposite direction, perhaps Roosevelt Lodge, parking at various "hot spot" viewing areas in the Lamar Valley along the northeast entrance road. Drivers and passengers, tightly bundled, climb out into mornings that can be frosty even in summer, cups of

coffee and spotting scopes in hand, exchanging quiet greetings with people they met in this very same place just yesterday, or the week before, or the week before that. Meanwhile those not yet ready to greet the day, mostly younger children, snooze away in the cars under blankets, soon to be roused as the first wolves or even grizzly bears come into view. By mid-morning the crowd will thin somewhat, only to reassemble for yet another hard look later in the evening.

Biologists have hardly been the only ones watching wolves in Yellowstone. So too have come visitors by the thousands, some for literally months at a time, creating what can only be called a full-blown wildlife-watching phenomenon. Almost from the beginning summer was a busy time for wolf watching, especially in the Lamar Valley, and within a couple years the winter months had grown more popular, too. Now at the ten-year mark the so-called shoulder seasons—those months sandwiched between summer and winter, and historically the slowest time in Yellowstone—are also drawing crowds. It's truly a world community, with people arriving not just from across America, but Canada, England, Germany, Portugal, Sweden, Norway, Japan, Australia, and Italy.

Amazingly, some 20,000 people are seeing wolves in Yellowstone every year, making it hands-down the best place on earth to observe these animals in the wild. As of this writing someone, somewhere in this national park has spotted a wolf 1,422 days running. To put this into context, Rick McIntyre describes a good day of wolf watching in Alaska's Denali National Park, where he spent fifteen summers, as seeing a single wolf for five minutes perhaps three miles away, only to then have it disappear over a ridge. "Compare that to Yellowstone," he says, "where for much of the year you can watch the same wolves over and over, often following them through their entire lives."

For those who've been peering through the spotting scopes, an unforgettable aspect of such encounters is the wolf's eyes, which can seem to look right through you. They are the eyes of something untamed, of a creature either unwilling or unable to divorce itself from the wild. On so many days we humans seem insatiable, determined to cobble together a fantasy in which there's nothing we can't have, can't own. But to a lot of wildlife watchers the wolf defies all that, standing as a link to the kinds of mysteries that lie well outside our pipe dreams of manipulation and control. Seeing a wolf in the wild can feel like one of the final frontiers of nature—a frontier that can never be possessed. What incredible fascination such meetings often bring.

By the time we were three years into the reintroduction the watchers were following wolves around like teenagers dogging rock stars. Stories were being traded—both about individual animals, as well as the histories of the packs. Observations became ever more sophisticated, organized so that whenever a wolf was spotted it was only a matter of minutes before those looking for them up and down the Lamar Valley coalesced. Almost everyone involved in this project has stories of seeing people break down in tears on seeing a wolf in their natural habitat for the first time. More than a few have declared the experience to be among the most important of their lives.

At the same time numerous dignitaries have come to Yellowstone to see wolves, including President Clinton, Secretary of the Interior Bruce Babbitt, Montana congressman Pat Williams, and George W. Bush's 2000 campaign manager, Joe Albaugh, not to mention directors of various government agencies from around the country. So too have come celebrities, from Tom Brokaw to Cameron Diaz, from Ted Turner and Jane Fonda to Sheena Easton and Ed Asner, from *Sports Illustrated* supermodel Rebecca Romijn-Stamos to rapper DMX. In truth it seems we're always fielding calls from people of note who want to see wolves. Many later tell us that the chance to watch wolves in the wild, an experience that somehow feels exceptionally real, gave them a much-needed respite from the distractions of daily life. Rapper DMX, or just "X" as he's often called, was stunned on coming to Yellowstone and seeing both grizzly bears and wolves. "I didn't even know this existed," he told me, going on to say that he loved it, that the experience changed his entire point of view.

Having come from what was for the most part solitary research on Isle Royale, walking five hundred miles to see maybe a single wolf, at first I tended to avoid the buzz and clutter of Yellowstone's roadside gatherings. One day, though, I was out with the crowds in the Lamar Valley, when sure enough a wolf began crossing the road. (By this time we'd figured out the main crossing zones for the animals and had closed them to human entry, not even allowing vehicles traveling the highway to stop.) The excitement was building. As I peered through my spotting scope something in the foreground caught my eye. A man in a wheelchair was the closest person to the wolf, and as the animal crossed the road it paused to gaze directly at him, offering one of those rare, altogether unforgettable feelings of being connected to the wild. From where I stood I could see what the encounter meant to him. He was truly moved. And that, in turn, moved me. From that day on I've been much less of a snob about roadside wolf watching. Here were wolves giving back to people, sharing with us something that seems increasingly precious in this exceedingly prescribed, prepackaged world.

Not just tourists, but people I meet throughout the year, from every walk of life, have shown a deep fascination for wolves. In 1997 I was in Dillon, Montana, to capture a rogue wolf pack that had been killing sheep in the area. As it happened a biologist on the Beaverhead National Forest had come on board to help; he took to the work easily, ultimately helping us to process five animals. As we loaded the wolves for the trip back to Yellowstone he asked me to please call him should we ever need more help. It had been, he said quietly, one of the five best days of his life. The return trip to Yellowstone meant first driving to the Dillon airport, where we'd staged the capture operation. On first arriving I'd been on the receiving end of some less than enthusiastic comments from locals, grumbling loudly about "them sons-of-a-bitchin' wolves." After the capture, though, with wolves actually in tow, some of the same men were falling all over themselves trying to get a look. I paused for a few minutes to give them a good view. The scorn and the sneer had gone right out of them. "Wow, would you look at that one . . . Look at those eyes—they look right through you, don't they? . . . Hey, that one's wakin' up!" It was much like what had happened when we first brought wolves through the park from Canada. While transporting animals in their shipping containers people ran up and posed beside the crates, asking to have their photos taken—this, even though the wolves weren't visible, caged behind aluminum slats. Like them or not, these animals have proven themselves a wild version of highly charismatic people, lives of the party at every party they attend.

For the past many years, key to a lot of people's wolf watching experience has been Rick McIntyre—the masterful Pied Piper of the wolf watchers, a volunteer for part of the year, then a project employee in seasonal months—who is unlikely to miss even a single day in the field. Rick adds important structure to wolf watching events, controlling in largely unseen ways crowds of well-meaning people who can get totally caught up in the frenzy—forgetting that wolves are wild animals, oblivious even to traffic on the northeast entrance road. I remember one cold winter night having dinner with him near my home in Gardiner, Montana, on the northern edge of the park, when a nasty storm blew in and snow began to fall. Rick refused all offers to stay over, even though reaching his home on the other side of Yellowstone meant crossing the park in truly awful weather. The Druid Peak Pack had been missing, he explained. He was counting on driving home through the Lamar with his radio collar receiver on, maybe catch the signal that might announce their return. Only then would he feel fully prepared for the next day of wolf watching. Stationed at Silver Gate, Montana, along the remote northeastern corner of the park, he's been known to go months without driving to town. Even getting him to park headquarters for meetings can be trying, as he's reluctant to miss a single moment when something might happen with the wolves.

"Imagine if you were a historian," Rick offers. "And by some strange circumstance you had the chance to go back in time and be witness to a really important era, maybe spend time next to Abraham Lincoln in the White House. Think of all the things you'd want to learn about, the questions you'd want to have answered." When it comes to American conservation, he believes this wolf reintroduction will be seen by future generations as having enormous significance. Rick says that on most days he has the old phrase *carpe diem* running through his head—seize the day. "This is an incredible privilege," he explains. "I'm always aware of that, always motivated to be here." As of this writing Rick's compiled just under 4,000 single-spaced pages of field notes on the Yellowstone wolves—three times more material, he points out, than found between the covers of the Bible.

He sometimes compares his enormous popularity with wolf watchers to what it might've been like to be a tour guide in London in the 1960s, helping people catch glimpses of the Beatles. "Where else could a government employee be so warmly received?" When I visit him in the field, always with crowds of people around, one of his favorite pranks is to use his telemetry receiver as a "bureaucrat finder"—waving the antennae wildly, letting it come to rest near where I'm standing, then adjusting the receiver so it screeches loud with feedback. "Looks like we found one," he quips. Beyond making sure things stay orderly in the melee of wolf watching, Rick provides us with vital information about individual wolves and pack sizes, as well as wolf interactions with elk, grizzly bears, and coyotes. He regularly spots for us during capture operations, often calling in wolf locations at first light.

Not surprisingly, the economic impact of wolf watching has been impressive. Studies prior to the reintroduction estimated wolves would bring in annually about twenty-three million dollars to communities surrounding the greater Yellowstone ecosystem;[1] though we can't yet affix a firm figure to it, early signs are that the numbers may be bigger still.[2] Several new businesses have sprouted up to serve the demand for guides, while a few old ones on hard times have discovered an eager client base for wolf watching safaris. (It's worth noting that in the Boundary Waters Canoe Area, some outfitters sell out dogsled trips based on a guarantee not to actually see a wolf, even to hear one howl, but merely to see a track.) Of course most wolf watchers stay in motels, eat out, and end up buying everything from warm clothes to spotting scopes to souvenirs—often at times of year when visitors have traditionally been few and far between. As Mike Phillips points out, the idea of gray wolf recovery in Yellowstone—which has been around since the 1940s—started gaining a lot of steam in the 1980s. By 1992 the handwriting was on the wall, and certain forward-looking businessmen moved to take advantage of it.

But not everyone's pleased. A primary engine of the former wolf-free economy was hunting on national forest lands surrounding the park, and some people maintain wolves will all but ruin that. Compared to hunters, they complain, who are known to lay down thousands of dollars for a week-long elk hunt, wolf watchers aren't big spenders. Yet there are still plenty of unknowns about all this. We've no clue, for example, how many fewer people are actually coming to hunt because of a perceived loss of game. Nor can we say how many sportsmen are day hunters, taking cow elk in winter, compared to the more costly quest for bulls in autumn. Then there's the not-inconsequential matter of hunter success rates. How different were these rates in the years before wolves returned, compared to elk hunting operations elsewhere? Does a decline around Yellowstone actually render the harvest more similar to other places in Wyoming, Colorado, and Montana?

Still, there can be another downside to having wolves so visible. The most easily seen wolves in the world, after all, are also the ones most exposed to people. So far we've been lucky, having had only four animals displaying what could be called habituated behavior—pulling food from garbage cans, walking toward people instead of away from them, circling cars stopped on the roadways. Thus far every habituated wolf we've seen in Yellowstone has been a young animal with time on his hands. The chores of the pack—defending territory, mating, killing elk, reinforcing the social hierarchy—tend to fall on the shoulders of older animals. A young wolf with everything provided for him, at the bottom of the pecking order, may out of a combination of curiosity and boredom decide to occupy his time with a little people watching.

It's certainly true that wolves almost never attack people. Throughout the twentieth century there were just sixteen reported cases of biting people, not one of which resulted in a death.[3] Most of these involved wolves being fed, which over time can make them lose some of their natural fear of humans. (Six of the bites mentioned above were on the Alaska pipeline, where workers were routinely feeding wolves handouts from their lunches.) We know Yellowstone visitors have given food to wolves on at least two occasions, though of course the real number is probably a lot higher. One time people were seen pulling up to two animals on the side of the road and tossing food out; as the wolves approached the driver snapped a couple photos and hurried off. Wolves crossing roadways may also walk by people, and some watchers have had a hard time resisting the urge to move in close for pictures. At other times a pack might make a kill at night close to the road, which by first light begins to draw crowds. On the plus side, people like Rick McIntyre—as well as increasingly knowledgeable visitors—are helping us keep people at safe distances, sometimes moving to observation knolls slightly farther away in order to not influence wolf behavior. Such caution can seem even more important when you stop to think that a young wolf in the Lamar Valley could conceivably end up dispersing to locations outside the park—lands with small towns and livestock and pets. Helping a wolf maintain its wariness here in Yellowstone might be what keeps it alive in years to come.

There's a great riddle about all this that people like to chew on now and then over cups of coffee: why are wolves by nature afraid of people in the first place? Any one of them, after all, could make short work of any one of us. In the course of my own work I've actually driven a mother wolf from her den to reach the pups—an intrusion she met by hustling away with her tail tucked between her legs. I also once mistakenly approached a kill before the wolves were finished with it, only to see the entire group scurry off in fear. Such cautious behavior may be related to the fact that we've long been killing them, thereby ingraining a level of cultural fear. Wolves on Isle Royale have been protected for over fifty years, yet they still flee whenever they see a person. On the other hand, in some remote locations where wolves never experienced persecution they show little fear of people, often coming very close. Yet they also show no aggression, seeing humans as neither prey nor threat.

Habituation is slow to develop, and the first thing we'll do with a wolf losing its sense of caution is to watch it carefully, noting its behavior. At the same time we try to make sure responsibility for staying separated isn't laid entirely on the wolf—that the people are also behaving. It should go without saying that one should never closely approach wolves, avoiding them whenever possible. And of course feeding them—or any other wild animal, for that matter—is about as blatantly irresponsible as you can get. If a wolf continues to show habituated behavior we'll first harass it in a way that doesn't cause injury—typically with rubber bullets or loud, sharp explosives called cracker shells. So far, we've never had to go beyond this stage. In the end the offending animals left these risky behaviors of youth, becoming as adults far more wary. If necessary, though, our final step would be to remove the wolf from the wild by killing it. Again, if things ever progress to this point it'll surely not be all the wolf's fault. But the people who helped cause the behavior will be long gone, leaving the wolf to pay for the problem with its life. What's more, should a wolf ever bite somebody in this, one of the most well-known parks in the world, all the terror of Little Red Riding Hood—still clearly simmering in parts of the culture—will come flooding back.

Curiously, we've got a different situation around Yellowstone National Park headquarters at Mammoth, where hundreds of employees live. Here resides a fairly tame elk herd that spends much of the year in and around people—if not exactly for their company, then at least for the lawns they keep. In recent winters wolves have figured out that they can take these animals, and that's been a little disturbing to some of the residents. Typically the wolves move in under the cover of darkness, and on a few occasions people have looked out their windows to see the animals walking right through their backyards. Meanwhile the family dog either goes wild, or just as likely, turns strangely quiet and passive. Whether wolves in your yard is thrilling or deeply troubling depends on your perspective.

Several times wolves have killed elk close to these same housing areas, including once in the yard of the elementary school. Another time an elk was taken near a restaurant, leaving blood on the steps and sidewalk. Again, some people were excited, some weren't. The difference between this situation and those of our earlier discussion is that these wolves aren't habituated, choosing to always flee at first light or with any sign of humans. The park's response has been to inform residents how to minimize the chances of an encounter: being careful with food; understanding that because dogs can be perceived by wolves as potential rivals it's important to keep them on a leash and bring them in at night; not to run if approached by a wolf.

◆ ◆ ◆

EVEN IN THE research community, not everyone's pleased about how easy it is to see wolves in Yellowstone. Veteran Canadian wolf biologist Lu Carbyn once commented that Yellowstone has changed the face of the wolf mystique. It used to take tremendous effort to see a wolf, he explained, and now here was Yellowstone, where a person could drive out and find them anytime he wanted. Lu seemed to be suggesting that something was lost, that making the experience of wolves an everyday occurrence, as opposed to something rare as it had been in the "old days," wasn't necessarily a good thing.

Many of North America's best biologists have a great keenness for the wolf research conducted from roughly the late 1930s through the 1970s—an era defined both by an unspoken passion for the wolf itself, as well as by a string of hearty, patient men willing to make long and determined treks by snowshoe through the remote lands of Canada, Alaska, Minnesota, and Wisconsin. Men like Sigurd Olson and Adolph Murie; Durward Allen, Dave Mech, and Doug Pimlott; Lu Carbyn, John Theberge, Rolf Peterson, and Paul Paquet; Vic VanBallenburghe, Robert Stephenson, George Kolenosky, and Gordon Haber, to name a few. It was a time of strong traditions. A period when "wolf meetings" consisted not of two or three hundred people flocking into a convention center, as happens today, but rather a small cadre of biologists huddled around a wood stove in some remote cabin in the North Woods. My own professional work with wolves began toward the end of this era, and as a young upstart I was well aware of what a privilege it was to be standing in such proud company. Yet even with all that, I'm more convinced than ever that the visibility of Yellowstone's wolves is by and large a good thing. In fact from where I stand, this unpredicted visibility seems arguably one of the best reasons to have brought wolves back.

The vast majority of what people experience of nature these days, after all, comes from television. And maybe it's there where Lu's concerns are most fully realized. Entertaining, and even educational, as it may be, television flattens wildlife watching—purging the physical discomforts, removing all the time normally spent waiting for something to happen. Every inconvenience is left behind on the cutting room floor. The result is often a kind of tepid album of greatest hits, a non-stop string of events that even most of us working in the field see only a handful of times in our lives. While it's true that wolves show themselves frequently in Yellowstone, their appearance is nonetheless still in the context of the larger wild preserve—uncut, unedited. A person has to at least be willing to make direct contact with nature, to experience an unfolding of life that goes far beyond the animal he's come to see. In that sense wolf watching in Yellowstone is an experience of nature much as it's always been.

It's hard to deny that many people who've thrilled to seeing wolves in Yellowstone will go home a little more thankful for the wild tapestry of life still sprouting across the American West. Some will even come to understand that if you care about wolves, then you absolutely must care about things like winter range for their primary prey base, the elk, which outside of federal lands is being lost at a frightening rate. Wolves, in other words, for some are the way "back in" to the kind of relationship with nature long considered a fundamental aspect of American identity. As best-selling nineteenth century author Henry George pointed out, the wild preserves of the West are critical, even for those who never set eyes on them. The mere thought of them, he suggested, tends to engender "a consciousness of freedom." To that end the memory of wolves running like the wind through the Lamar Valley, or sliding down snowfields in fits of play, or even sleeping away a summer afternoon in the tall grass, can be a remarkable touchstone to that which makes our lives and our culture just a little more fascinating, a little more rich with wonder.

Number 14, right

Portrait of a Wolf

NUMBER 14

S HE WAS THE YOUNGEST and least known of what we sometimes call the heroine wolves, the mystery of her life deepened by having lived in some of the most remote lands anywhere in the Lower 48. Her number was 14, a member of the Soda Butte Pack, so named for a nearly extinct hot spring vent standing near their release site at the east end of the Lamar Valley. Number 14 arrived in the second of two wolf shipments from Canada that took place in 1995 (as did Number 10, who joined 9 and her yearling daughter at Rose Creek), carried to the pen with little pomp or fanfare. Unlike 9, who blessed the ecosystem with eight little ones in May of 1995, only one of 14's pups survived that year—a female known as Number 24, born northeast of Yellowstone in the rugged folds of the Stillwater Canyon.

It was the following year, though, when her life took a major turn. In 1996 she denned on a private 13,000-acre ranch north of Yellowstone Park, near the small village of Roscoe, Montana. She and her mate, Number 13, were in many ways model citizens, never once preying on livestock, despite there being an abundance of it all around. Even many of the ranch cowboys were fond of her, one commenting to me that it was really nice to see her out there with the elk. Some of the neighbors, though, thought otherwise. After receiving numerous death threats to the pack we made the decision to launch yet another capture effort, re-locating what had by then grown to four adults and four pups, in hopes they'd find homes on less contentious ground. This time, rather than the pups being squirreled away in a jumble of talus, as 9's offspring had been, they were deep inside a burrow. To retrieve them, Mike Phillips crawled into a dark hole with flashlight in hand—an intrusion the little ones, at this point about six weeks old, met with their game faces on, growling and being just as fierce as they could be.

Once back in Yellowstone for the summer—again, placed in an acclimation pen to cool whatever urge they might have to run back to the same place—we set them free in October of 1996. Their new home was to be a long ways from just about everything, along the wild and remote southeastern arm of Yellowstone Lake. Helping us out that day was then-director of the U.S. Fish and Wildlife Service, Jamie Clark, who'd been a good friend to the late Mollie Beattie. Indeed Jamie pretty much picked up where Mollie left off, both having proven them-selves strong supporters of wolf recovery. After working long and hard on a never-ending list of bureaucratic challenges in Washington D.C., Jamie found the hands-on labor of turning wolves loose into the wild enormously satisfying.

For a good year the eight-member family thrived, with 14 giving birth in 1997 to a litter of pups near the shores of beautiful Heart Lake. By this time 14's mate, Number 13, was well past old age. Even at the time of initial release he sported a coat that had gone from black to a bluish-gray, leading us to nickname him "Old Blue." He was also extremely cautious. While still in the acclimation pen, at the first hint of our approach Old Blue was the only animal to make a beeline for the safety of one of several doghouses we'd placed in the pens. Given that shy nature, we were a bit dumbfounded when on release he suddenly gained his courage, displaying all the confidence of an alpha male. By February of 1997, though, Blue was often seen struggling behind the pack. The next month his collar began emitting the fast, steady signal we call mortality mode, or just "mort mode," indicating that he'd finally died. The life expectancy of a wolf in Yellowstone—without factoring in pup mortality—is 3.4 years; Old Blue blasted that average out of the water, making it to the wholly ancient age of 11.9. (On average females live four months longer than males; the longest lived females we know of are 7 and 42, who lived to be eight years old, though that record may soon be broken by two wolves born in 1996—44 and 48—still going strong.) Though we didn't yet know it, shortly before his passing Blue had bred with 14 one last time.

Following the death of her mate, in a move no scientist I've ever spoken to has ever seen or heard of, 14 simply took off. Leaving her home territory at Heart Lake, parting from both her pups and yearlings (this in itself is extraordinary), she wandered westward through the snow, crossing terrain so inhospitable it contained not a single track of another animal. Through a combination of tracking from the air, as well as actually following for miles her prints on the ground, we finally located her on the Pitchstone Plateau—standing alone on an empty, windblown slope. She halted momentarily, peering at the airplane as we circled, then simply resumed her journey, traveling west for another fifteen miles. Shortly afterward our tracking record grew incomplete, leaving us unsure just where she roamed. After about a week she returned to her own territory, reuniting with her family. Though no one wanted to say 14 traveled alone so far because she was mourning the loss of her mate, some of us privately wondered.

Normally we try to retrieve the carcass of a wolf right away, thereby giving ourselves a better chance of determining the cause of death. But Number 14 and her offspring remained very close to the place where Old Blue died, denning in a nearby cave in April of 1997—one of the few such den sites in all of Yellowstone. Not wanting to disturb the pack we waited—months, as it turned out, until the family finally left the area the following August. As you might guess, by the time we recovered Old Blue's radio collar there was little left of his carcass. Yet his radio collar was well chewed—a sign, perhaps, of what may have been his last contribution to a litter of teething little pups.

Following 14's long sojourn the pack carried on, though without their alpha male. A lack of snow in the fall of 1997 put a major delay on the annual elk migration down from the high country, the herds not fleeing the weight of winter until well into December. When the snows finally did come that year, and the elk began moving southeastward toward the park border, the Soda Butte wolves moved right along with them—in the process crossing into territory occupied by the Thorofare wolves. Not surprisingly, that intrusion led to a battle. While at eight animals the Thorofare Pack had numbers equal to Soda Butte, only two of their wolves were adults, compared to four mature animals in the trespassing pack. With the odds clearly in their favor the Soda Butte wolves first killed Number 35, the Thorofare alpha male. Later, walking around the site, following tracks and studying the blood-soaked snow, we began piecing together the fight. Number 35 had been caught on the ice along the shores of Yellowstone Lake, eventually coming to a log where the wind had sculpted snow into a small cavern. It was here he made his last stand, crawling into the cavity and using it as a kind of backstop. It must have been a grisly battle, as evidenced by the fact that we found nothing but hair, urine, and blood; the alpha's radio collar lay on the snow, no hint of the wolf that wore it. This lack of remains left us wondering if the Soda Butte wolves consumed him, though that would be rare, as typically wolves don't eat their rivals. I was so intrigued by the scene that I later returned on horseback, trying again to locate some sign of 35. There was nothing.

While Thorofare's alpha male was being dealt the death card, his mate and the rest of the pack were on the run, heading south, at one point turning up Escarpment Creek. It was a place we'd never seen them before, and probably with good reason, given that the drainage dead-ends at the base of a 10,000-foot plateau known as the Trident. Perhaps because they were unfamiliar with the terrain, at one point the wolves traversed a narrow chute, triggering an avalanche. When the rumble finally stopped alpha female Number 30 and a lone pup were gone, swallowed by a river of snow. A week later we visited the site, digging into debris well over our heads—all the while hearing the radio collar beeping somewhere below in the icy rubble, but never managing a recovery. The following summer we rode in on horseback some thirty-two miles from Ninemile Trailhead, finally locating their skeletons at the foot of a small waterfall, shrouded in the lavender blooms of harebells.

With one brief, fierce battle Number 14 and the Soda Butte wolves had managed to claim a territory of massive proportions, stretching some forty miles from the southern shores of Yellowstone Lake all the way past the park's southern boundary into the Bridger-Teton Wilderness. It was the largest territory of any wolf pack in the ecosystem. While in summer two or even three groups of wolves could sustain themselves here without much trouble, so harsh is the region during cold months that all but about two hundred elk leave for friendlier winter ranges—some heading to lands located south and east of the park, others traveling northeast all the way to the Lamar Valley.[1] During the winter of 1998 the Soda Butte wolves (eventually renamed the Delta Pack) made a trek to the National Elk Refuge just outside Jackson Hole, Wyoming, where typically some five to ten thousand elk are found. They lingered for a while but chose not to settle in, even though one of the packs in that area was headed by 14's daughter, Number 24—the lone little pup to survive back in the spring of 1995 in the Stillwater Canyon. For reasons only they can know 14 and her kin instead headed back to those inclement lands of southern Yellowstone, where they would spent most of the next several years.

Calamity struck again in April of 2000. On a routine tracking flight along the south edge of Yellowstone Lake, near where 14 had been released after being removed from that ranch near Roscoe, Montana, we found her dead, a golden eagle already on site and beginning to feed on her body. Bedded down nearby were her pack mates, one of which was an adult male we're quite sure had bred with her, bringing the promise of pups to the pack for the first time since 1997. A hundred yards away was a dead moose, partially consumed. Examining the carcasses, putting the clues together, it seemed clear that both predator and prey had died in the same great battle. Number 14 was six years old. On a later overflight our pilot saw a grizzly bear covering her body with debris, as bears will often do to keep scavengers away, protecting the carcass as if it was his own kill.

We discussed hiring a helicopter to retrieve her, as we did with the Thorofare wolves that had died in that earlier battle—both to confirm the circumstances of her death, as well as to see if she was pregnant. But we were unlikely to learn much from such a recovery trip, given that scavengers had already begun to consume her, obscuring the forensic details. Much of my reason for wanting to go get her was sentimental. Besides having known her intimately since her arrival in Yellowstone, this was a wolf that spent much of her life roaming the wildest, deepest reaches of the ecosystem. Many a time in winter I'd watched her leading her pack, usually some forty or fifty feet ahead of the next animal in line, steadily pushing through the deep snow. It was hard for me to lose her, to let her go without knowing the details of what had happened, quite possibly to never find her remains. In the end, though, I simply couldn't justify the trip.

The following summer I climbed aboard my horse, Amos, and headed for the Delta to find what was left of her. Not surprisingly, little was waiting for me but bone and hide. I found too the dead moose she'd been battling with, also entirely consumed by scavengers. Yet the trek proved worth the effort. Examining the scant remains I discovered that since the last time I'd handled 14 she'd broken her leg and it had mended itself. The bone hadn't healed straight, there was a slight bend to it now, but it was nonetheless solid. Watching her numerous times from the airplane I was never able to detect anything wrong with her. I knelt one last time by her tattered carcass, feeling the quiet of this extraordinary spot in the Yellowstone backcountry. A slight breeze came up, fingering the tall summer grass. Looking around, all in all it seemed a beautiful place to come to rest.

Wolves 44 and 126, both born into the original Soda Butte Pack in 1996, are still alive deep in the heart of Yellowstone. At this point we can barely hear the radio signal coming from 44's collar, picking it up only when the plane is directly above her. But we do hear it now and then. She struggles on, one of the oldest wolves in the population, somehow still able to make a living in these lonely folds of the Wyoming backcountry. Meanwhile 126 went on to succeed Number 14 as the alpha female of the Delta Pack, producing several litters of pups of her own. Now in her elder years, we're uncertain whether or not she still holds that top position—a question that's hard to answer, given the remote lands these wolves call home.

Originally of the Chief Joseph Pack, wolf Number
113 helped formed the Agate Creek Pack. Today
he continues to serve as the group's alpha male.

The Swan Lake wolves are unusual in that they are one of only two packs in the park (Nez Perce is the other) with all gray wolves.

Above: All wolves reintroduced into Yellowstone were first acclimated for ten weeks inside chain link enclosures. This helped break the animals' natural inclination to head back north, searching for their Canadian homes.

Left: We captured this 130-pound wolf, a member of the Swan Lake Pack, in November of 2003. Unfortunately, his radio collar failed within the week.

A Nez Perce wolf being released into the acclimation pen.
All of the original Yellowstone wolves were transported from
Canada in aluminum crates, and each was radio collared.

Druid Peak wolves in Lamar Valley. The rich
wildlife resources of the valley—in particular,
the great Northern Range elk herd—have made
this a hotbed of wolf activity.

Carter Niemeyer and Doug Smith working on two
Swan Lake wolves during collaring operations.
Besides receiving radio collars, the animals are
measured and a small amount of blood is extracted.

Collaring a wolf is just the beginning. The real
work is tracking the animal from the air—in this
case, through the remote lands of the Thorofare.

Helicopter darting operations in the
Lamar Valley. The two wolves are
members of the Druid Peak Pack.

Targeting a wolf from
the Cougar Creek Pack
for darting. I'm fully
outside the door, with
my feet on the helicopter
skid. I'll not be able to
take the shot, however,
until the helicopter is
much closer.

Mollie's Pack (formerly known as Crystal Creek Pack), live in the Pelican Valley. Over the years, deep snow and little prey has caused the size of the pack to wax and wane. As of early 2005, it may be breaking up completely.

Top left: Wolves and coyotes have never been on good terms. Here wolf Number 21, alpha male of the Druid Peak Pack, digs into a coyote den.

Bottom left: Despite the wolf's superior strength, this coyote can't resist nipping the tail of Number 21, hoping to deter him from further digging into the den.

Above: Even a wolf only has so much patience.

A face-off between a grizzly and a wolf from the
Delta Pack. While grizzlies generally dominate
wolves near killed prey, if the bear ventures near
a pack's den, as this one has, the wolves are much
less willing to give ground.

The Swan Lake wolf pups by their den,
early on a July morning. Looking on is the
pups' mother, alpha female Number 152.

A rare shot of a wild
wolf nursing her pups.
The mother is Number
7, alpha female of the
Leopold Pack from
1996 through 2002.

A common escape strategy of elk being chased by
wolves is to run into water. In this case, an elk pursued
by Mollie's Pack has entered Pelican Creek during spring
snowmelt. Every wolf that tried to get near was swept
away in the current.

Exactly why some wolves jump in and swim after
elk, while others don't, remains a mystery.

The graying alpha male of Mollie's Pack, Number 193, and his yearling son, 343, have killed a bull elk, only to see it quickly taken over by a grizzly. Most kills made by this pack in the Pelican Valley are commandeered by grizzly bears.

This sow grizzly is taking these four Mollie's Pack wolves very seriously. So far we know of three grizzly cubs that have been killed by wolves.

Wolves aren't random hunters, but selective. By first
running prey animals, a wolf can examine them for
vulnerability. Most such chases do not result in a kill.

When elk stand and face wolves, or even charge them, they are rarely killed.

Alpha wolves are the most dominant members of the pack. Shown here are the famous Numbers 42 and 21, alpha male and female of the Druid Peak Pack, along with two subordinates.

Wolves are impressive runners, able to achieve
speeds of up to thirty-five miles per hour.

Here in the Lamar Valley, coyotes have learned to keep
their distance. Wolves easily dominate the smaller animal,
having triggered significant declines in coyote populations
on Yellowstone's northern range.

To guard against wolves and other predators, mother elk often hide their calves in tall grass or sage. A wolf's diet isn't focused exclusively on these calves; rather, they will be taken as the opportunity arises.

Agate Creek wolf Number 113 attacking a cow elk. While wolves typically attack prey with the help of other pack members, the animals also sometimes make kills on their own.

A Druid Peak wolf decides to test a herd of elk.

With little snow on the ground this bull elk
has good footing, so has decided to stand
his ground before these Druid Peak wolves.
He was not killed.

Two wolves overtaking
a cow elk. The neck is
a common attack point
when trying to bring
down a cow elk, while
the more dangerous
bull elk are typically
struck from behind.

 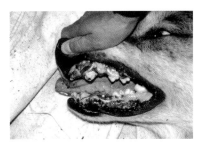

One of the surest ways of determining the age of a wolf is by its teeth. White teeth with no staining, in perfect condition and with no breaks, usually indicate a very young wolf.

Wolf Number 13, about ten years old when this photo was taken, was the oldest wolf brought from Canada to Yellowstone, and it shows.

For the wolves of North America, gray is the most common color phase, as shown by these two members of the Swan Lake Pack. They can also be either black or white.

It's October 2004, and the Leopold Pack takes one of its first jaunts with all the pups in tow. Travel is difficult in this long grass, as the pups—still full of play—simply don't want to follow.

The Yellowstone Wolf Project could not succeed without a remarkable collection of staff and outside experts. Pictured above are (clockwise from top): Gerald Mernin and Michael Ross; Mike Phillips; Ed Bangs, Douglas Smith, and Michael Jimenez; Kerry Murphy; Roger Stradley; Rick McIntyre; Dan Stahler; Rolf Peterson; Debra Guernsey (center).

CHAPTER 7

THE
WOLF EFFECT

If we had to name the most important scientific aspect of Yellowstone wolf research, it would likely be the challenge of finding out what these animals mean to the functioning of the ecosystem as a whole. Wolves were of course part of the region long before Europeans arrived on the scene, which means most of the life here was well adapted to having them around. Yet the science we've conducted over the past decades has been on

lands bereft of wolves. In that sense Yellowstone offers the best chance we've ever had to figure out the difference between a wilderness system with wolves versus one without them (a so-called "time series" experiment). And for those of us working as scientists, that's an incredibly exciting thought. Naturally, central to this notion will be the wolves' impact on elk. Not just directly, though, through killing for food, but indirectly from the fact that the mere presence of wolves changes both how elk are distributed, as well as how they behave. And as those things change, it will inevitably lead to changes in the environment as a whole.

Wolves are often described by the term "apex carnivore," which simply means that they sit on top of the food chain. (This food chain is also sometimes referred to as a food web. That name refers to the fact that if you map out all the connections that exist between organisms in a given ecosystem, you end up with a figure that looks much like a spider web.) In simplest terms the sun fuels the food chain through plants, which are then eaten by consumers like elk, bison, deer, etc. Those consumers, in turn, are eaten by wolves, cougars, and other carnivores, which are eventually themselves eaten by decomposers. In this way the energy from the sun can be said to cycle through the system. By sitting at the top of the food chain wolves and certain other carnivores tend to have significant effects on the life around them. Those impacts can sometimes tumble down the entire chain all the way to the plant community—meaning the animal is affecting things indirectly, as well as directly—a phenomenon that lies at the heart of what scientists call a trophic cascade.

Whether or not wolves have started a trophic cascade—which, by the way, is a process so complex it's not yet well studied—remains one of the most hotly debated topics in all of Yellowstone. Though we've got several seminal pieces of research to lean on, proving the extent of a particular animal's effect on the surrounding ecosystem is a hard thing to do, especially in big areas like Yellowstone, where interactions between wolves and prey and vegetation are remarkably tangled. Nonetheless, with the return of wolves it took little time before this national park became a crucible for such research, with competing teams of scientists vying with one another to be the first to document critical discoveries.

So far the focus of this work has been on the northern portion of the park—as noted earlier, a vital area for thousands of ungulates, including the northern Yellowstone elk herd. Because the large quantity of prey animals have made this region by far the busiest for wolf activity, if a trophic cascade is going to happen anywhere, this is the place. So far these studies have been looking at three woody species: cottonwood, aspen, and willow. While in truth these plants cover only about 2 percent of the northern range, scientists see those sites where they occur as biological hot spots, highly significant to a variety of animals. To put it simply, any recovery that gets going in these plant communities is going to affect lots of players.

A good example is the beaver. Biologist Dan Tyers reintroduced beavers adjacent to the park in the Gallatin National Forest shortly before we brought back wolves; since then those beavers have migrated downstream into the national park, able to settle in Yellowstone because of ongoing willow recovery. (While Dan's reintroduction no doubt sped things up, this recovery probably would've happened anyway. Beavers have long occupied the Yellowstone River, and would've surely migrated into the park as willow became available.) I've personally been involved in Yellowstone beaver surveys since 1996, when there was one beaver colony on the entire northern range of the national park. In 2003 there were nine colonies, occupying sites in Slough Creek, the Lamar Valley, and Swan Lake flats.

From what we know so far willow recovery seems connected with wolf reintroduction, the rebound starting roughly two to three years after wolves were released. More impressive still, this resurgence began not when there were a mere 4,000 elk in the northern herd, as there were in 1968, but when there were 14,000. (The lower number in 1968 was due to ranger control actions, designed to reduce what was considered an over-abundance of elk.) Admittedly, we have to be careful when making such associations—a kind of scientific shorthand known as correlational science—since in the end only actual experiments will prove the case. Those experiments are now ongoing, as is computer modeling, mostly done by outside researchers looking at everything from willow regeneration to seed production, from the effect of fire to the influence of beavers, elk, and moose.

With the beaver have come beaver ponds—rich, vibrant oases providing habitat for insects, fish, amphibians, reptiles, small mammals, birds, even moose. Likewise the area immediately surrounding beaver ponds and streams, known as riparian zones, are home for a number of plants and animals unable to exist anywhere else. Research in similar environments at other natural areas—one south of Yellowstone in Grand Teton National Park, as well as in Canada's Banff National Park—offers strong evidence of the connections between riparian zones and various songbirds, including yellow and Wilson's warblers.[1]

Any amateur naturalist walking into the northern range with an eye to what's going on with willow would in no time at all figure out that the recovery isn't uniform. That's more evidence still that wolves are involved. After all, if willow growth was the result of a landscape-based effect—something, say, related to climate change—we'd expect to see it everywhere. But the spottiness of the recovery is possibly because it's happening in those places where elk have learned they're at higher risk of being killed by wolves; once aware of this the elk simply don't spend their time in such locations, or not nearly as much as they used to. And it's in exactly those areas that willow is coming back. While the exact nature of such relationships isn't yet known, nearly everyone agrees that elk are behaving differently, and willow is returning.

Not that the wolf is the only piece of the willow puzzle. Work by Dr. Dan Tyers has shown that the number of moose declined significantly following the massive fire season of 1988, primarily due to a loss of critical forest-based winter habitat. (In those places not burned in the 1988 fires, there are today just as many moose as there were before.)[2] Given how much moose eat, less moose certainly couldn't hurt the cause of willow regeneration. Yet if these animals were a primary factor, why didn't the recovery begin earlier, closer to the time when moose populations plummeted after the fires? Furthermore, we don't yet understand if willow is being helped simply because of fewer moose, or also because moose, like elk, are changing their behavior in the face of wolf packs.

Plenty of attention is also being given to cottonwood and aspen, both of which were declining on the northern range. So far cottonwood recruitment seems to be on the increase since wolf reintroduction, while nothing observable is happening with aspen—at least for now.[3] (That said, many researchers feel it's only a matter of time before recovery will be observed in both species.) Meanwhile Douglas Frank of Syracuse University in New York said on a recent visit that he was beginning to see a wolf effect on park grasses. On so-called high risk sites—areas with poor visibility, where it would be hard to spot an oncoming wolf—grass production increased. These results are only preliminary, but they're yet another part of trophic cascade research worth watching.

Still another kind of trophic cascade playing out in Yellowstone stems from all the carcasses wolves are leaving behind. Even if a pack is big enough to eat nearly all of the prey animal they kill, there'll always be morsels left behind for other scavengers. (To a degree we can actually correlate the size of wolf packs to how big their major food source is. Wolves that kill deer, for example, live in packs of five to seven, while elk-killing packs typically range from eight to twelve.

Moose- and bison-killing packs will often be fifteen-plus animals strong.) Thus far we've observed no less than twelve different species using prey killed by wolves, including ravens, magpies, bald and golden eagles, and coyotes.[4] Biologist John Varley has dubbed this phenomenon "food for the masses." "In all the planning, all the studies," says Varley, "the one thing we totally underestimated was how many other mouths the wolves would feed. Beetles and flies and mountain bluebirds—I mean this is incredible."

Biologist Dan Stahler and noted raven expert Bernd Heinrich have been spending time watching ravens following wolves, the birds knowing full well that if they stick around long enough they're going to get a meal. In virtually every case, ravens are at a wolf-kill site as soon as the prey animal falls. As Heinrich once told me, ravens have a hard time pecking the eye out of a dead squirrel, let alone opening up a 700-pound dead elk. Here they can have the wolves do it for them. In one remarkable scene, some 135 ravens were seen on two adjacent kills. (The average wolf kill attracts 29 ravens.) As part of ongoing research Stahler and Heinrich compared the birds' reliance on wolf-killed carcasses to situations where meat was supplied artificially. Basically the two men hiked around placing on open ground the legs from elk carcasses. The ravens didn't bite. Some would fly over and do a double-take, but in the end they just kept going. On wolf kills, though, the birds started feeding immediately. Stahler and Heinrich's conclusion, based on a solid understanding of the raven's habits, was that these birds are extremely cautious about approaching unknown food sources. While feasts being offered by humans are suspect, meals made courtesy of wolves or other predators is comfortable, well-charted territory.[5]

Magpies too are eager to take their own turn at wolf kills, sometimes being the first to a carcass, though never by much. So too will eagles eventually come, as well as both black bears and grizzlies—at least when they're not asleep in their dens. For all their power, grizzlies lack the speed and agility needed to regularly take adult elk on their own. Yet as noted earlier, a grizzly can usually command a wolf kill at his pleasure, in the process gaining food that may prove critical to his survival. In Pelican Valley, one of the densest grizzly bear areas in the park, virtually every kill the wolves make is stolen by grizzlies. It's not a matter of *if* the bears will come calling after a kill, but *when*. In one case in the Pelican Valley a bear biologist observed twelve grizzlies and four wolves on a wolf-killed elk. On several occasions I've seen four to six bears descending on a wolf kill, and in one extreme case, watched dumbfounded as a large grizzly on a wolf-killed elk fended off twenty-four wolves. Time after time individual wolves mustered the courage to approach the kill, only to be met head-on with an angry charge. Afterward the bear always returned to lie on the dead elk, determined to protect every morsel.

For the most part wolves are to bears what mosquitoes might be to the rest of us—pesky annoyances. Wolves dart in and out with abandon, even sit on their haunches six or eight feet away from the bear, looking calm, knowing full well the bruin lacks the quickness to ever catch them. Several times I've seen a bear lurch and swipe at a wolf harassing him, but a wolf can leap out of harm's way in the blink of an eye. If wolves encounter a bear on neutral ground, with no kill around, they may—though not always—hassle it in a half-hearted manner and be on their way. The intensity of the interaction increases if a food source is involved. The harassment reaches the highest level only if the bears wander near the wolves' dens or rendezvous sites, where pups are vulnerable. At those times several wolves will dart in and out all at once, clearly more antagonistic, as often as not biting the bear on the butt every chance they get. Even with this sort of insult the bears usually don't bother going after the wolves, knowing it's a hopeless cause. More often than not they seem to simply grow weary, and finally amble away. (Grizzly cubs, though, are more vulnerable; so far we've been able to document three of them having been killed by wolves. Because of this, mother bears are less inclined to challenge wolves for carcasses.)

The meat wolves leave behind becomes especially important to bears in autumn, when they're driven to put on as much fat as they can before the big sleep. For decades there've been only a few really good sources of food for bears in this season, one of which is the nut crop of the whitebark pine. But beyond the fact that whitebark pine stands are declining throughout Yellowstone, victims of both changing climate and a disease called blister rust, the other problem is that these trees produce nuts only sporadically. One season may offer a bumper crop, only to have next year's harvest be a total bust. We now have reason to believe that in those lean years especially bears are turning to wolf kills. In fact the highest number of grizzlies ever seen on wolf kills—not just in the Pelican Valley, but throughout the park—was during a fall when the nut crop completely failed. Lastly, so too are these carcasses important to bears at the end of winter, when they emerge from dens ravenously hungry

While grizzlies have the luxury of approaching wolf kills with impunity, not so with the coyotes who come calling. When much of your normal diet consists of mice and ground squirrels, the sight of several hundred pounds of elk meat must be awfully hard to resist. Yet coyotes have to exercise tremendous caution, given that wolves frequently kill them at both den sites and on carcasses—so many, in fact, that since wolf reintroduction the coyote population on the northern range has declined by half.[6] It's unlikely wolves will eliminate coyotes altogether, as they did on Isle Royale, but this smaller canine will probably never again have the place in the ecosystem that it did prior to the wolves' return. This in itself may not be a bad thing, given that prior to the wolf reintroduction Yellowstone supported one of the densest coyote populations in all of North America.

Coyote-wolf interactions provide yet another great example of the fact that you can't pull on one strand in the web of life, without it being felt someplace else. Some researchers think red foxes, which are commonly preyed on by coyotes, will make a strong comeback in the years to come. Likewise coyotes are major predators of pronghorn antelope fawns, taking them in that period before they're old enough to run with such blazing speed—when the only strategy is for their mothers to hide them. Working in conjunction with pronghorn researcher John Byers from the University of Idaho, we've found that the areas with the highest pronghorn fawn survival rate are located near wolf dens. Wolves rarely prey on pronghorn fawns, apparently having better things to do than spend their time hunting up their hiding places. And for their part coyotes wisely avoid wolf dens like the plague. Loss of coyotes could also lead to an increased availability of rodents, since these make up the canine's primary food source. If rodents increase, it might bode well for other animals that like to eat them, including hawks and owls. Though right now it's impossible to say, we may one day discover that along with all the other changes wolves have ignited, they may also be indirectly responsible for an increase in raptors. This coyote-rodent connection has been documented around wolf dens in nearby Grand Teton National Park by researcher Brian Miller, though more testing needs to be done.

Some people who aren't particularly fond of wolves have made the comment that even without them the scavenger community was doing just fine, what with hunters being counted on to shoot elk and deer every fall. But there are big differences between the remains of hunters and those provided by wolves. For starters, wolves leave carcasses laying around at all times of the year, across nearly the entire landscape.[7] Human-related leftovers such as gut piles, on the other hand, occur only in fall, and at clumped locations. Still other people have suggested that there's plenty of food being left by other scavengers, in particular the cougar—a predator that's actually a more efficient killer than a wolf. (On average one wolf kills an elk about every fifteen days, while a cougar takes one every week.)[8] But cougars are solitary hunters, and as such have evolved to cover their kills in order to make them less available. I saw this play out vividly one day from a place called Hellroaring Overlook, where a cougar and a pack of six wolves had each killed an elk, roughly a half-mile apart. The wolves had eaten and were bedded down sleeping, ignoring the ravens and magpies swarming around their kill. The cougar, meanwhile, was frantic in the face of these interlopers, diving and dashing in a desperate attempt to chase them away.

The wolves' strategy is basically to out-eat the birds—make a kill and then try to consume it right then and there. Though not proven, some researchers speculate that the reason wolves live in packs in the first place is just for this reason, to out-eat scavengers.[9] Generally speaking, in Yellowstone it takes about ten wolves to consume most of a carcass, leaving behind only small pieces of meat.[10] Above ten wolves and some animals in the pack aren't going to get enough to eat; below ten, and scavengers will consume the leftovers. But being alone cougars simply can't eat the whole kill in one sitting, instead staying on it for days, maybe even a week. In those times when the animal isn't actually eating the carcass stays buried, keeping others from getting to it. By all indications the strategy works. Observation has shown very little use of a prey animal killed by a cougar other than by the cat that killed it.[11]

So far all we've talked about are vertebrate scavengers. But once all the aforementioned animals have had their turn—and several others not mentioned—the invertebrates take over, especially beetles. And what the beetles don't get leaches into the soil in the form of nutrients— so many nutrients, in fact, that a study on the Konza Prairie Reserve in Kansas found that carcasses contributed more nutrients to the soil than did either feces or urine.[12] While this hasn't been tested enough to be universally accepted, it seems likely that the kills wolves leave on the landscape are a solid source of nutrients for the functioning of the system. All of this simply because wolves killed an elk. In that sense the death isn't merely an end, but a beginning. The diversity wolves help support means a healthier, more resilient system. "If we have all the parts of this ecosystem," says John Varley, "then, as Aldo Leopold said, it should function better. To the extent we're able to know, the wolf has restored the prehistoric and historic biodiversity of Yellowstone. And in all the Lower 48 states, this is the only little scrap of land where that claim can be made." Indeed, if we're to take seriously the long-standing policy of the National Park Service to restore natural conditions, it would be hard to imagine a better way to achieve it than through the restoration of the wolf.

◆ ◆ ◆

OVER THE PAST several years, perhaps the biggest mental challenge for those of us involved with this project has been grappling with claims that wolves are wholly responsible for declines in the northern Yellowstone elk herd, which now stands at roughly ten to eleven thousand animals—down from nearly twice that in the early 1990s. Adding fuel to the fire was scientific research from 2002 documenting drops in the survival rate of elk calves—known as the "recruitment rate"—a trend suggesting that elk numbers may at least in the short term stay lower than they were a decade ago.[13] But historically we've always seen great fluctuations in elk numbers in Yellowstone—even when no wolves were present. What's more, population monitoring suggests the decline of the northern elk herd began well before wolves hit the ground.[14]

It's not that wolves don't play a role in such fluctuations, because they clearly do. But they're just one part of the story, along with factors like drought, harsh winters, and human hunting. As discussed, seven out of eight elk herds in Yellowstone leave the national park every winter, at which point most are fair game for hunters. But beyond all that, there's something strange about this sudden panic over a declining elk herd. For more than three decades, from 1932 to 1968, elk were regularly hunted by park rangers in order to protect the resource from overgrazing and overbrowsing; with the end of those artificial control actions, along with the discovery of new wintering areas north of the park, by 1992 the population had swelled to a staggering twenty thousand animals. Those high numbers spurred great criticism from both the public as well as some segments of the scientific community, who worried that too many elk were damaging the ecosystem. In part as a reaction to those concerns, in 1995 and 1996 Montana Fish, Wildlife and Parks increased the number of cow permits given to elk hunters— a move expressly intended to initiate population declines. How amazing, then, that within just a few years—for no other reason than that wolves are now in the picture—the debate switched from having too many elk in the ecosystem, to having too few.

In addition to wolves coming back to this landscape, in the past fifteen years other major predators have been on the increase. The population of grizzly bears—a major consumer of elk calves—is considerably higher in 2004 than it was in the early 1980s, as is the number of cougars, which again, have a significantly better per capita kill rate than do wolves. In all today there are six major elk predators in greater Yellowstone, forming a multi-carnivore system that will continue to exert a strong influence on their prey.

Another significant factor influencing elk populations is weather and climate. One example is the calamitous winter of 1988–1989, following the catastrophic fires of the previous summer, which burned some 36 percent of the national park. (The 1988 fires, by the way, were an enormous event here in Yellowstone. Hundreds of thousands of acres burned. Smoke poured into the sky, making the normally clear, brilliant days of late summer dark and murky and full of soot. For a time, at least, what had been cool, shaded stands of living conifers were changed into a patchwork of blackened trunks rising out of knee-high, nutrient-rich grasses and forbs. Yet nature reclaimed the world lost in that season in remarkably short order. Except for the age of the timber—and therefore the density, since young trees grow more compactly than do old ones—in most places today you'll find the very same plant communities as before the burn. So far as we can tell, in the grand scheme of things the fires had little effect on the business of being a wolf.)

Even more significant was the winter of 1996–1997, in Yellowstone one of the most severe of the entire twentieth century. Heavy snows in November and December made it tough for elk and other ungulates to move around and find forage. Then around New Years, typically a very cold time, it started raining, followed soon afterward by temperatures plummeting to well below zero. The heavy snow, then rain, then extreme cold turned the snow pack to concrete, sealing off grasses under a hard shell of ice—a catastrophic situation for ungulates. Before long both elk and bison began leaving the park in huge numbers, with thousands of elk dying along the way. Nor would many of their calves make it through the winter. Meanwhile fleeing bison were being rigorously monitored—part of an agreement with the state of Montana to prohibit them from leaving the park, due to fears of spreading a disease known as brucellosis to the region's cattle. Out of a population of 4,000 bison some 1,400 died that winter, 1,100 of them shot at the park boundary.

As for the wolves, in late winter of 1997 it seemed they couldn't kill enough elk. Indeed, this was the only year we've documented so-called surplus killing, which refers to wolves taking more than they can immediately eat. Even so, as we continued to watch those carcasses over the next few weeks, many of which did in fact still have meat on them, we saw wolves returning to feed a second and even third time. In truth some reports of surplus killing stem from people surprising wolves on a kill and thus driving them away, then being incredulous about how little they consumed. Despite a sordid mythology that paints wolves as bloodthirsty killing machines, in the vast majority of cases a wolf taking everything he can means just plain getting enough to keep going. For every hunt that leads to a kill a pack endures many times that number of failed attempts; in Yellowstone proper, only one out of every five attempts is successful.

As critical to declining elk numbers as the winter of 1996–97 was, possibly more consequential was the record drought that followed— one that by some indications was as bad or worse than the dust bowl of the 1930s. At first the milder winters with less snowfall actually helped ungulates. The low snow pack made travel easier, thereby allowing greater access to forage. But over time low precipitation—especially during summer, when both the quality and quantity of grass is set for the rest of the year—is a major stress factor.[15] Had such conditions lasted only a year or two the system would've adjusted. Most soils do tend to store moisture, after all, besides which many grasses are remarkably resistant to drought. But we're talking six years of it—one of the longest known dry spells on record.

Current computer analyses suggest that given the recent severe drought, significant declines in the northern range elk herd would've occurred even had wolves never been reintroduced. Research by the wolf project suggests that wolf predation has been compensatory, which basically means prey animals killed by one cause—in this case, wolves— would've died anyway because of being severely stressed by other factors. Another way of saying it is that a wolf taking one animal means another will survive. Had drought not occurred, on the other hand, wolf predation on elk may well have been additive mortality, meaning that each elk killed probably would have lived had wolves not killed it. (Some other research models, though, indicate that most wolf predation has been additive.[16]) While predicting the cycling of elk populations is a terribly complex task, there seems little doubt that if all the above-mentioned factors occur simultaneously—from weather and climate stresses (including severe winters coming back-to-back), to liberal hunting policies, to high levels of predation—elk may well decline to even lower levels than they are now. Yet by all indications, a drought of the magnitude seen over the past six years may trump everything else, becoming the most important life factor not just for elk, but for virtually every other plant and animal in the ecosystem. (A count done in early 2005, incidentally, showed the population of the northern elk herd to be at levels similar to the previous year.)

Taking the long view, such declines in elk will no doubt be temporary. While it's true that high ungulate populations can overharvest the food supply, especially in drought periods, thereby leading to greater mortality from all causes, the animals that make it through are left to enjoy greater abundance. That, in turn, eventually leads to an increased survival rate in calves. This isn't to say that with a fully restored suite of predators elk will be as plentiful as they were before. But changing the dynamics of the ecosystem by bringing back its top predator doesn't diminish the ability of that system to persevere. Generally speaking, the idea that elk would disappear in the face of wolves being back in the landscape flies in the face of the two species having co-existed in relatively stable fashion throughout the northern Rockies for thousands of years.

Portrait of a Wolf

NUMBER 7

ONE OF THE MOST noteworthy events marshaled by those first wolves released in 1995 was the formation of the Leopold Pack, created by a pairing between Number 2 of the Crystal Creek wolves and Number 7 of the Rose Creek group. This would prove the first naturally forming wolf pack in what we now call Yellowstone's New Wolf Era; as a way of commemorating the event we named the group after Aldo Leopold, the brilliant scientist who first recommended wolf reintroduction to Yellowstone in 1944. Leopold, considered by many the father of modern day wildlife management, was even wiser than many give him credit for, fostering the notion that predators had value long before it was a popular idea even among biologists. "A thing is right," Leopold claimed in his classic work, *A Sand County Almanac,* "when it tends to preserve the integrity, stability, and beauty of the biotic community. It is wrong when it tends otherwise."

Number 7 had left her mother and stepfather, Number 9 and 10, almost immediately after being released from the acclimation pen. For the next ten months she traveled as a lone wolf, making her own kills, thriving. Then on Blacktail Deer Plateau she paired with Number 2, who'd split from his own pack only a month before. That match created tremendous excitement not just among those of us working the wolf project, but in park staff as a whole. On first sighting them I snapped a photograph—a lousy one, it turned out, mostly due to the uncontrollable excitement I was feeling at the time. (For all the thrill, this pairing did cause some concern given that we'd just built an acclimation pen on Blacktail to hold two wolves, Numbers 35 and 36, which at that point were ready for release. With 2 and 7 having settled the area naturally we had to find another place for these other animals, finally letting them go in the Lone Star Geyser Basin.) The pairing of 2 and 7 marked nothing less than the beginning of wolves expanding successfully on their own. Even better, their choice of homes on Blacktail Deer Plateau was a great location for observing, allowing us to easily record their comings and goings.

In their first year together the Leopold wolves had three pups. Amazingly, Number 7 was out killing elk only days before giving birth—a significant feat, though one that wouldn't have been necessary had she been in a larger pack with helpers at her side. The pair chose to excavate a den on Blacktail Deer Plateau at a site we still call the den forest, but used it only one year before moving to another location. This second den site has been used six out of the past nine years; even in

2003, the first year Number 7 was no longer the breeding female of the pack, the new alpha female continued to use this den—a great example of how tradition plays out in wolf culture.

During their stint as alpha wolves Numbers 7 and 2 would produce seven litters totaling thirty-four pups, at least twenty-nine of which managed to survive past the age of one. Two of those offspring went on to form the nearby Swan Lake Pack, as well as the Cougar Creek Pack. Yet another pup grew up to become a key member of the Rose Creek Pack, meaning that he dispersed back to his mother's group of origin. Through much of 2004 the territorial boundaries of the Leopold wolves were among the least changing of any in the Yellowstone ecosystem. They never left Yellowstone National Park (from 1995 to 2003 only four packs could make that claim), and their pack size was extremely stable, fluctuating over six years between eleven and thirteen members. While in that same era the alphas of other packs were producing multiple litters, 2 and 7 faithfully bred only with each other, with no breeding activity outside the alpha pair. Curiously, after these two wolves died the size of the pack swelled to nineteen members, then twenty-four by late 2004—by far the largest ever recorded for the group. Just as the Rose Creek wolves rose to prominence with twenty-four animals on the northern range in 1998, followed by the Druid Peak Pack at thirty-seven members in 2001, the Leopold wolves may well be the next power pack of the region.

Despite their phenomenal run as alphas, the end for these founding members of Leopold came somewhat abruptly. In May 2002, Number 7 was killed by the neighboring Geode Creek wolves, a new group forming after the break-up of the massive thirty-seven member Druid Peak Pack. When we found her carcass it was evident that not only had she given birth to a litter of pups that year—at the time of her death they were about a month old—but that she was still nursing, being several weeks from completing her weaning. Yet thanks to the communal, family-driven nature of wolves, other females from the pack were quick to come on board and care for the pups—not nursing them, since these other adults wouldn't have been lactating, but still providing food. All eight survived. As for 7's partner, Number 2, after losing his dominant status in the pack he died in much the same fashion as did his mate, on the last day of 2002, falling at the jaws of the Geode wolves.

To signify this changing of the guard we now refer to this group as Leopold II. They continue to use the same territory, frequenting the same haunts the original pack established back in 1996. If history is any teacher, our best guess is that wolves will remain in this exact place for many years to come.

CHAPTER 8

THIS FEAST OF

SCIENCE

To the extent we can ever paint a rich and meaningful portrait of a wolf's life, we have to first understand that its very existence turns around markedly different behaviors at different times of year. Wolves at this latitude breed in February, giving birth in April after a gestation period of about sixty-three days. From that time on the animals will spend their summers

anchored either to the birthing den or, beginning about a month later, to aboveground, den-like locations called rendezvous sites. The sole event that allows the group to finally transition out of this somewhat rooted period to the highly free-ranging behavior we see through winter is the physical maturation of the pups. As soon as youngsters are capable of traveling with the adults, typically in September or October, the pack begins to move as a unit.

While as researchers we invariably end up juggling a variety of investigations, what drives much of our work has to do with figuring out the exact nature of the relationship between wolves and their prey. Historically, across North America this has been one of the most controversial wildlife management issues ever considered, reflecting the fact that wolves have a lot of influence on prey animals that we humans tend to want for ourselves.[1] During the early phase of this project I polled wolf biologists across the continent, asking what they thought would be the most important study task we could undertake, both during and after the initial releases. A clear majority said we should monitor kill rates. In other words, most scientists felt it vital to determine how many prey—or more specifically, the amount of meat ingested per wolf—was occurring over a specific amount of time.

With this in mind, the first thing we did was set up a study to determine what kind of prey wolves were choosing, as well as how often they managed to actually make a kill. The idea was to answer that question posed by the scientists at two different times of year: first in early winter, when prey animals are healthy and usually difficult to bring down, and then again in late winter, when the prey is a lot weaker, and therefore far more vulnerable. Once again we turned to Isle Royale for ideas. Every year since 1958, from January through early March researchers there have flown out to the island to carefully monitor wolf-moose interactions. These flights, which occur every day the weather permits, have as one of their main goals to find wolf kills—a task made easier both because moose are large, so the wolves spend a lot of time on each kill, but also by virtue of the fact that midwinter thaws on the island are rare, which makes it much easier to snow track from the air.

But conditions are a lot different in Yellowstone, where mountains and forested ravines make it difficult to track animals from overhead. What's more, winter thaws are much more common here, and along with gusty winds can make snow tracking difficult. Throw in several thousand ungulates, which in their own comings and goings often end up erasing many of the wolf tracks, and you can see that emulating an Isle Royale study—especially without radio collars—would be incredibly challenging, if not impossible. Still, we used the pearl of the Isle Royale idea, flying every day the weather permits, spending much of our time looking for kills.

Given that we couldn't sustain the more than two months of flying currently being done at Isle Royale, our next task was to come up with a workable research schedule. To help with this part of the equation we turned to the Brooks Range of Alaska, where biologists Bruce Dale and Layne Adams had come up with the idea of monitoring wolf killing activity through thirty-day study periods, flying every day possible for a single month.[2] Because we needed snow on the ground to aid us in spotting kills, we decided the early winter study should take place from November 15 through December 14, while our late winter period would go from March 1 through March 30. Just as on Isle Royale, we named these intensive research periods Winter Study, and they've become an enormously important part of our program. During the course of these periods we try to reach every wolf kill, except the extremely remote ones, traveling by foot, ski, or horseback, thereby gaining a lot of details not evident from the air.

A backbone of our work—here, as with wolf studies in other places—is fixed-wing aircraft, in particular that tried-and-true airplane of the far northern bush, the Piper Super Cub. Capable of carrying only a pilot and passenger, the Super Cub is for starters inexpensive to operate. To put it in perspective, flying a Super Cub costs us around $125 per hour, compared to anywhere from $700 to $1,400 per hour for a helicopter. First built in 1952, the model we use (PA-18), is unique among airplanes for the almost unmatchable lift provided by the wing. It's highly maneuverable at slow speeds, can make tight circles, and has proven so safe at low elevations that some people know it as the poorman's helicopter. For all these reasons, probably more North American wildlife research is done from Super Cubs than from any other airplane. Some pilots are so enamored of the Super Cub that it's the only plane they'll fly, leading them to be known by the moniker "Cub Pilot."

Given how astonishingly visible many of Yellowstone's wolves are from the ground, we also monitor kills by stationing observers there. Actually, packs living close to the highway in the northern portion of the park have proven so easy to watch that observers can determine whether or not they have a kill on an almost daily basis. This information is ultimately compared with that gathered by the aerial crews. Using both sets of statistics we then apply a fairly complex mathematical equation to help adjust for human error, as well to more closely estimate the likely number of kills neither ground nor aerial crews were able to find.

If this all sounds like a lot of work, it is—far more than the government has money to pay for. For this reason each year we assemble an extraordinarily dedicated team of volunteers—nine people for each and every Winter Study. Without their assistance, we couldn't pull off the project. Almost to a person these people dedicate their hearts and souls to the task, giving themselves over to hard work in bitterly cold conditions, the hours often spanning daybreak to dark. Prior to each Winter Study we provide a three-day training session, during which knowledge gets transferred from experienced volunteers to those newly hired. This mix of new and old helpers goes a long way in assuring the data is gathered with a high degree of accuracy. (It takes a person about one Winter Study to really get the hang of it; thankfully, most who come stay on for more than one season.) We've never once advertised for these positions. Word of mouth, mixed with the intense interest many people have in wolves, has proven more than enough.

What we've learned about wolf kill rates so far—that question so many biologists were curious about—is that on average Yellowstone's wolves kill 1.4 elk per wolf per month in early winter, and 2.2 elk per wolf per month late in the season, for an average of 1.8 elk per month across the course of a winter. This means a group of ten wolves—the average pack size in Yellowstone—takes an elk about every third day in early winter and one about every other day in late winter. (Curiously, while from 1995 through 2000 the kill rate on the northern range showed exactly this kind of increase across the winter season, since 2000 such swells haven't occurred. In other words, for some reason the wolves are eating less than they used to. Supporting this finding is the fact that the weights of the northern range wolves, especially pups, are declining, while in the park interior weights are holding steady. As of yet we have no idea why, though we're speculating it might have something to do with the region's prolonged drought.) Finally, our preliminary research during summer months, combined with results from other studies, suggest wolves eat roughly 25 to 35 percent less at that time of year.[3]

Crunch the numbers and you end up with a grand total of about 180 to 190 elk being taken every year by each ten-member pack on the northern range. If we assume that interior wolf packs kill about the same number of elk that the northern range packs do—and we think they do—the number of elk killed every year across Yellowstone would be 3,000 to 3,200. This represents roughly 9 percent of the summering elk population, currently estimated at about 35,000 animals.[4] Again, these are ballpark figures. Pack sizes vary, and summer kill rates have not yet been well studied.

Besides having learned a lot about how many prey animals wolves take, we've also gained a better understanding of how they go about it—knowledge earned from actually watching them interact with elk and bison. Once again, initially we didn't think such insights would be available to us, given that elsewhere in North America wolf attacks on prey are rarely witnessed. In his thirty-five years on Isle Royale, for example, Rolf Peterson has seen only six kills.[5] Compare that to the past decade in Yellowstone, where collectively we've seen more than a hundred. For starters, our observations confirmed what other studies elsewhere have suggested, which is that wolves manage to actually make a kill only about 15 to 20 percent of the time.

Most wolf researchers feel that as wolves travel they also hunt. How much energy they put into that hunting, though, depends on their level of motivation. If it's not been all that long since a wolf fed, the desire to kill again will be fairly low; still, stumbling across a vulnerable prey animal may lead to a half-hearted attempt at making a kill. The hungrier the wolf gets, the more energy it will give—and the more risk it will take—for the chance to gain a meal.

In all probability wolves carry a kind of territorial map in their heads, knowing full well which places on their home ground are likely to provide the best hunting opportunities at various times of the year. What's more, their noses are easily good enough to allow them to detect prey from several miles away. On first encountering a prey animal wolves often just watch them (indeed, that may be all they do), looking for any sign of vulnerability. For their part, any elk within eyeshot will often go from a state of casual attention to a heightened state of alert only if they see a wolf showing signs of actual hunting. Sometimes that means wolves dropping into a low, half-crouching posture, but more often it has to do with more subtle clues, rules of the game that are difficult for most of us to even perceive. Either way, this tendency of prey animals to not react to wolves unless they're really a threat is critical when it comes to conserving energy. In winter especially, any animal that bolted at the mere sight of a predator would have a hard time surviving.

If the encounter does escalate beyond a spectator sport, the wolves will approach the prey, interacting with it as a means of testing. (Indeed, it's helpful to think of each state of a wolf-prey encounter as an ever more stringent test to determine vulnerability.) Still, even as things grow more intense, the encounter is as likely to simply end as it is to lead to an attempt at a kill. Often when wolves approach prey will run from them, which can result in a chase—what we call an attack. Sometimes, though, the prey animal won't flee (this is especially common with bison), preferring instead to stand its ground. By all indications, this is a great strategy for rebuffing a wolf attack. Making a kill is a lot harder for a wolf when a prey animal is facing it, with its strong kicking legs and sharp hooves—and in some cases, horns or antlers—poised and ready, than when its legs are otherwise occupied in running away. In November 2004 I watched three wolves attacking a herd of about 200 elk. One cow elk not only refused to run but actually charged the wolves, at which point they merely jumped out of her way. As the chase unfolded the fleeing herd cycled back around a few times toward this cantankerous cow, and every time the wolves chose to give her a wide berth. Clearly, they wanted nothing to do with her.

As the attack continues to escalate the wolves may pick out either a group of fleeing prey or a lone individual. Again, what they're doing comes down to a matter of testing, trying to target only catchable animals. Once a prey animal is targeted, the wolves may or may not attempt to actually capture it. In fact many attacks end right there, as the wolves realize the prey is healthy enough to outrun them. If it is vulnerable, though, the wolves may attempt to take it by trying to sink their teeth into the prey animal and then hang on. A wolf's canines are especially well suited for such a task. The base of these teeth are elliptical—as opposed to round, like a cat's teeth—which allows them to withstand extraordinary amounts of forward and backward force without breaking.[6] While of course such an event is no picnic for the prey, it can be brutally hard on the wolves, too, since sinking their teeth into a running or kicking prey animal can result in broken ribs or legs, cracked skulls, even death. I've seen wolves that were hanging on a prey animal stepped on, kicked, flung into the air, and slammed into logs. Wolf 174, a former alpha female of Mollie's Pack, badly injured her front foot while attacking a bison. I watched her limp for months. For a time she wouldn't put any weight at all on the foot, yet at the moment the pack encountered an elk or bison they wanted to kill she was right there, trying her best to help. I was amazed at her dogged tenacity, despite what looked to be a severe wound.

After painstakingly analyzing several hundred wolf attacks in Yellowstone, researcher Dan MacNulty found that wolves attempting to kill prey animals tend to display six behaviors, or "states."[7] These are: search, approach, watch, attack, target, and capture. These states can vary in their order, be repeated, or even come to an end only to start up all over again, at least until the wolves finally see what they need in order to move in for a kill. And again, most of the time it's the prey that wins.

As we've suggested, when it comes to wolves selecting prey, elk are clearly the animal of choice. Yet depending on the season, a wolf's diet may broaden to include several of the other seven ungulates that live either full-time or seasonally in Yellowstone. Wolves in the interior of the park especially may take bison, though for the most part this happens in late winter, when that thoroughly imposing creature is typically at its weakest. It takes a lot of winter to wear bison down enough so wolves can actually kill them, and even then the battles are fierce, often lasting the better part of a day. On at least one occasion a bull bison has killed a wolf and severely injured a second. Twice we've seen wolves thrown through the air like sacks of potatoes—once courtesy of a bison's horns, the other by means of a hard kick from a hind leg. Yet by late winter Mollie's wolves, for example, will be taking on average a bison every week. Again, the strategy wolves employ for tackling any large prey—be it bison or moose, bull elk or musk ox—is to avoid the front of the animal, where it's all too easy to be kicked or gored by an antler or horn. The vast majority of attacks by Yellowstone wolf packs on bison are focused on the hind quarters.

There are also moose to be had in the national park, though over the past decade we know of only about three dozen actually falling to wolves. Moose too are formidable, with cows weighing in at about a thousand pounds, and bulls tipping the scales at roughly 1,400—seven and ten times the size of a large wolf, respectively. Mule deer, meanwhile, tend to migrate out of the park for the winter, though in summer they can be found in sufficient numbers for wolves to make at least an occasional meal. Right now mule deer make up just under two percent of a Yellowstone wolf's winter diet, while in summer that climbs to twenty-five percent—a figure we determined by studying scats found around den sites. There are relatively few white-tailed deer in Yellowstone, and so far we've failed to record a single one being taken by wolves. Finally, we know of wolves taking only two bighorn sheep and two mountain goats, that low number reflecting the fact that both of these creatures can easily scamper across terrain completely unnavigable to most predators.[8]

No matter how many different prey animals might be available, wolves typically have a "primary choice" (which again, in the case of Yellowstone, is elk). What the wolves might do if the day comes when their first choice isn't so readily available is one of the hottest questions in the park today. Some research suggests that as the primary prey base declines wolf numbers will decline right along with them—the prey numbers leading the predators. Other studies, though, indicate that wolves may switch to other prey, focusing instead on their second choice. Of course this assumes not only that there are sufficient numbers of that second choice, but just as important, that the prey animals are actually vulnerable. In theory, at least, if wolves were able to successfully make such a shift their numbers might stay higher. And that, in turn, could allow them to continue to exert a bigger effect on their primary prey, the elk. Elk numbers might stay lower, in other words, than if predator and prey populations were dancing to the same ebbs and flows.

◆ ◆ ◆

As WINTER YIELDS to the warming winds of April, we begin paying special attention to those wolves giving birth to pups—a phase of research called den study. Seeing a wolf den is a pretty hard thing to do, so well concealed are they, and for some packs we never do manage to find them. Still it's important that we try, especially given the need to manage the area surrounding the sites in a way that protects the wolves from human disturbance. At present we have two self-operating telemetry systems that we place near known den sites, each meant to monitor the comings and goings of radio-collared wolves. Those without radio collars are kept track of, at least to a degree, by field observations, though these are applied only sparingly, to a few dens. The problem with such field work is that we run the risk of disturbing the wolves at a critical time in their life cycle. To reduce potential problems we never take up observation positions close to a den, using spotting scopes from locations often more than a mile away. (Such precautions aren't always followed in other places. On Canada's Arctic tundra, for example, where suitable den sites are limited and therefore predictable, some biologists conduct capture operations simply by waiting until wolves are denning.[9] Outside the scientific community, at least one canoeing guide service in the region specializes in finding wolves at their dens, then picking up the pups and handing them off to clients.[10] Research is ongoing to determine just how touchy wolves might be about such practices; so far, as with nearly everything else, the results are site specific and dependent on individual wolf personality.)[11] We're also interested in the phenomenon of wolves using the same den over and over, sometimes even after the death of the breeding female who excavated it in the first place, as we saw both with wolf Number 7 of the Leopold Pack, and Number 42 of the Druids. From what we've figured so far, about 70 percent of dens are ones used in the previous year.

With the coming of summer we start the business of counting pups. If finding dens is tough, laying eyes on young pups can be harder still. We're never quite sure if our counts are accurate—among other things, there can always be a pup or two hiding in the den while others are out frolicking—which means it's difficult to make accurate estimates of early pup mortality. Those we do spot are often in full-blown puppy mode, biting the tails of adults, wrestling with each other in great tumbles of fur, leaping into the air for no apparent reason other than it's a whole lot of fun. This penchant for play will continue well through the summer—from youngsters tossing pieces of carcass into the air and catching them like so many Frisbees, to entire families sliding down remnant patches of snow.

Well after the wolves have left their dens we go in to gather data—making notes about the basic characteristics of a given site, also gathering scat, or feces, which allows us to figure out what the wolves are eating in the warm months. (Given the overlap in size of coyote and wolf scats, wolf dens are the most reliable places for picking up droppings.) For me this is the season of hiking and riding horseback to far-flung locations, drifting through the magnificent valleys, plateaus and forests that comprise the Yellowstone backcountry; trailing along streams lined with monkeyflower and fireweed, watching for elk calves romping in the meadows, for the flash of red-tailed hawks.

Besides checking den sites and picking up scat, once a week we locate from the air all the packs in the park, tracking them by means of signals being given off by their radio collars. Among other things this allows us to examine differences in the use of summer territory versus winter territory, and through that, understand better how wolf life changes through the seasons. We know, for instance, that in summer wolves rarely travel together, instead moving singly or in twos or threes. This splitting up means locating collared wolves takes a lot longer in summer months than in winter, when the group tends to travel more as a single unit. Such loose organization reflects the kind of prey Yellowstone's wolves tend to eat during warm months; generally speaking, in that season comes a more mixed diet—deer, elk calves, elk, carrion, ground squirrels, and beavers—whereas in winter months the packs dine mostly on elk.

◆ ◆ ◆

NO DOUBT ABOUT IT, the wolf's shining season comes in the heart of winter. Warm months bring heat, of which they're not at all fond, as well as bugs and smaller amounts of food. And on top of all that, stronger prey. Besides, there's really no such thing as weather too cold for a wolf. During initial reintroduction activity, with the animals in transport boxes and the thermometer stuck at minus thirty degrees, they seemed completely unfazed.

A wolf's easy season, though, is for biologists the most challenging, in part because it's when we do radio collaring operations—typically in January and February. (Lately, given that the drought of the past six years has rendered midwinter no better for snow conditions than earlier in the season, in 2003 we darted seventeen wolves in the month of November. Likewise in 2001 we darted several in early December.) Initially every wolf reintroduced to Yellowstone wore a radio collar. After all, the thinking went, we literally had them in hand, and by collaring each individual we'd be better positioned to gauge the success of the reintroduction. Since that time we've reduced the number of collared wolves to between 35 and 40 percent of the population. Roughly twenty-five animals are collared each year, 60 percent of them pups. Being able to follow the wolves on a regular basis allows us to better understand their needs and behaviors, and through that, hopefully make more intelligent management decisions. Collaring remains an ongoing priority both because batteries wear down after a time, but also because there are always animals dispersing, some going on to start other packs.

We now have in place guidelines that prevent us from collaring more than 50 percent of the wolves in any given pack. In addition ear tags, while used in many wildlife studies around the country, are intentionally not used on Yellowstone's wolves. Both decisions reflect the fact that many visitors enjoy wild animals looking wild, with no evidence of humans having meddled in their lives. While we continue to place a high priority on gathering scientific information, so too do we need to be concerned about preserving the aesthetics of wild nature.

Make no mistake about it, catching a wolf isn't an easy feat. Just keeping up to date with collar losses through death and dispersal can be demanding. Capture's on my mind most of the year. On some days I look forward to it, but other times I dread it—not because of the work, but because of the stresses of wanting to do it safely, not to mention within budget. While flying around in a helicopter (used in conjunction with the Piper Super Cub), and then handling wolves offers great scientific opportunity, issues of logistics, weather, and general risk—not to mention the cunning nature of the wolves themselves—make for challenging days. Still, once aloft in the helicopter, strapped in with the door off and darting rifle in hand, scanning the wild landscape playing out below, I'm there a hundred percent. Picking out a wolf to catch, hearing the sound of helicopter blades ripping and clawing at the air—in those moments absolutely nothing else calls for my attention. And these days, that's a pretty remarkable place to be.

Once wolves have been chased by a helicopter during a darting operation they become awfully clever at avoiding us the next time. Which is why it's extremely hard to capture the same wolf twice. On top of that, helicopter darting was developed in the north, on lands without trees. But much of Yellowstone has plenty of timber, and at the point the wolves reach it they win—a fact they're clearly aware of. The Chief Joseph Pack especially shows uncanny skill at this kind of maneuvering; many a time I've hovered over them in a helicopter while they stood in the trees and looked up at me, seemingly defiant. On the other hand, we have as a goal to always chase the wolves as little as possible to achieve an acceptable degree of collaring. Not only do we want to avoid bothering wolves more than we have to (or, for that matter, provide them with a free education on how to avoid helicopters), but we also don't want to ruin for visitors the blissful quietude that is Yellowstone in winter.

With other capture methods like trapping, the animal may lie alone, sometimes for hours, before someone reaches it. Darting allows us to tend to it right away. When a gunner hits a wolf with a dart the helicopter immediately peels off, allowing the animal time to go down without any extra anxiety. Likewise, as collars are being placed around a wolf's neck, vital signs are continuously monitored. Nor will we leave an area until we know the animal is up and about again—a policy that sometimes requires leaving spotters on the ground some distance away, watching for the animals to rouse. People often ask if this kind of handling might result in wolves becoming habituated to humans, in turn causing them to get into trouble in nearby communities or on cattle and sheep ranches. But as we mentioned earlier, wolves aren't just naturally wary, but terrifically difficult to habituate. During darting operations, the only handling that occurs is when the wolf is sound asleep from the tranquilizer.

The systematic darting and collaring of wolves in Yellowstone began in 1998, nearly three years after the initial release. As a capture technique darting requires plenty of skill, the darter basically leaning out the open side door of a helicopter, secured by a harness attached to the frame of the aircraft. The movement of the machine tends to be erratic, subject to unpredictable jolts from ground winds, not to mention the swoop and wiggle that comes from the pilot trying to match the running of the wolves themselves. This is why, despite the best abilities of the man behind the dart gun, it's all for naught without an incredibly skilled pilot at the controls, able to follow a speeding, zigzagging animal determined to find cover. Even under ideal circumstances it takes a gunner roughly five or ten seconds to reload, allowing a wolf running at thirty miles an hour to cover more than seven hundred feet.

Wisely, the Park Service insists on lots of training to be certified as a dart gunner. I completed such prep in 1999 in a course involving live helicopter trials, taught by National Park Service wildlife capture specialist Michael Coffey. Shortly afterward I traveled to Alaska to work with Layne Adams, a veteran wolf darter of the U.S. Biological Survey. Well aware of the hazards that can come from getting overly excited, Layne treats the subject very matter-of-factly. Even so, the first wolf I ever tried to dart got away, basically because I forgot to pull the hammer back on the dart rifle. When I squeezed the trigger, nothing happened. The animal simply ran off into the trees. (The helicopter pilot nicknamed that wolf "Waterloo," then insisted on finding him for me another day.) It would be the first in a long string of lessons about the need to be able to think clearly in the wake of what's always a powerful rush of adrenaline—not to mention the occasional helicopter pilot yelling to "shoot now!" or offering not-so-helpful comments like "What happened? How'd you miss that shot?" I also learned a lot from U.S. Fish and Wildlife Service biologist Carter Niemeyer, who by the time

I got my feet wet had already darted several hundred wolves in the Lower 48. For a couple years we worked alongside each other, taking turns at the gun, routinely bantering back and forth about who was doing a better job and taking more difficult shots, a kind of friendly jabbing that allowed me to keep the pressure in check. Ed Bangs, wolf recovery coordinator for the northern Rockies, also was extremely helpful in the darting department.

Before actually climbing aboard the helicopter and putting my finger on the trigger of a darting rifle, I spent literally hundreds of hours flying in the spotter plane. Cruising some fifteen hundred feet above the ground, spotters—as mentioned earlier—are the eyes of the project, the ones who actually find the wolves for the darter. Spotters also keep a darted wolf in sight, so that when the drug finally takes effect the helicopter can easily find the animal, pick it up, and take it to the people responsible for processing. While all this is going on the plane also stays in touch with headquarters, calling in every fifteen minutes, allowing us among other things to keep abreast of developing weather.

More often than not, the pilot of that yellow Piper Super Cub in the skies above Yellowstone is Roger Stradley—not just a superb pilot, but so well attuned to every aspect of the operation that we long ago started referring to him as "General Stradley" or just plain "the General." Taught by his father, a World War II flight instructor, Roger's been flying Yellowstone since 1952 and knows so well every creek, lake, mountain, ridge, and plateau that long ago I stopped even bringing a map. At this point he's got roughly 50,000 hours in this type of plane, and the way he flies gives life to the old saying that you don't really fly a Super Cub, you strap it on. When weather moves in on us, especially wind, Roger has a handle on where he can go to get us out of it; some mountain passes or valleys work better than others, depending on the conditions, and he knows them all.

◆ ◆ ◆

OVER THE YEARS there's been plenty of excitement during collaring operations. I recall in particular November of 2003—a time of year in the northern climates I'd grown to love, when the occasional brilliant sunny day slips in between the gray and wind and cold. It was to be our earliest starting date for collaring operations, the previous record having been December 10. On our list of most wanted for the day was the Geode Creek Pack, which by that point was down to just one collar for the entire group. Other targets we were hoping for included members of the Mollie and Nez Perce packs—the latter wolves being especially challenging, given that they rarely presented themselves in places where they could easily be darted. Giving us hope on that first day was the fact that Roger Stradley, piloting the spotter plane, had found both packs out in the open—Nez Perce working the sprawling expanses of the Hayden Valley, and Mollie's in that part of the Pelican Valley not heavily forested.

At the controls of the darting helicopter was an outstanding pilot, Gary Brennan of Hawkins and Powers Aviation, working a Jet Long Ranger III—an aircraft with a lot more oomph than some other models, which I never appreciated more than when we were dangling a paltry hundred feet or so above the ground. We left the airport at Gardiner headed first for Pelican—eager to reach Mollie's wolves since only the two alphas of that pack were collared, and the batteries were getting old. Just as we were getting ready to leave, though, the General radioed from the spotter plane and changed plans, diverting us to the Hayden Valley to get the Nez Perce Pack instead. The call was confusing, what with to my mind Mollie's being the bigger priority, but radio transmissions are never a good place for lengthy discussions. Not only because words routinely end up cut or garbled, but because there's a need to not tie up the air waves. I'd learn later that fog had rolled into the Pelican Valley, making work there impossible; Roger's plan was to complete the collaring of Nez Perce first, at which point he hoped the weather in Pelican would improve.

This was my first darting trip of the year, so I was feeling a little rusty, full of early season jitters. While the Nez Perce wolves remained out in the open, I knew I'd have only one chance before they hit the trees, sending us back home to try again another day. Complicating matters was that there was only about an eight-inch layer of snow—not enough to slow the wolves down, leaving them fast moving targets filled with plenty of "juke and jive." Greyhounds, we sometimes call them in these conditions, speeding dogs that make landing a tranquilizer dart a tough proposition. Thanks, though, to some skillful piloting we quickly darted four members of the pack, including the old, grizzled-looking alpha female, Number 48, whose radio collar batteries were already dead. Also darted that day was Number 340, a two- to three-year-old female who later that winter would take off to form her own pack near Old Faithful, a group now known as the Biscuit Basin Pack. Yet when it came time to try for alpha male Number 72, whose collar also needed replacing, I missed badly.

By this time the fog had lifted in Pelican Valley, and we headed over to try our luck with Mollie's Pack. We knew this would be a different operation altogether; both alphas were old, all too familiar with the darting drill, which meant they'd waste little time hustling for cover. Sure enough, even before we entered the outer edges of the Pelican Valley they were up and running for the trees, all but two ignoring the hovering helicopter. One of those who paused for a second look was an enormous male, Number 194, last captured four years earlier, now wearing a collar with dead batteries. His sheer size reduced his capacity for fancy maneuvering, which allowed us to get a dart into him fairly quickly. The second animal was an uncollared pup, a lot more agile than big old Number 194, but whose inexperience led him to make the mistake of running into the open where we were able to quickly dart him. We called the General in the spotter plane and he told us that was it—there were no more wolves in the open. All things considered, not a bad start to the darting season.

The next day was a Saturday, but when it comes to these sorts of operations we have to work whenever weather is good and there's aircraft available. What we needed was one of those rare November gifts I'm so fond of—a clear day with low winds—which is just what we got. As usual, the General was out early, locating the Geode Pack in a perfect spot. We needed Geode. They were a key pack, living in the middle of wolves and grizzlies, with cougars, coyotes, elk, bison, and deer. Tracking them, in other words, would allow us to learn not just about their movements, but about how they were interacting with these other species. As of that morning we had only one member of the pack collared, alpha female Number 106, who we'd caught the previous year. (Number 106, as you may recall, had been a low-ranking member of the Druid Pack during that fateful brawl between Number 42, the so-called Cinderella wolf, and her super aggressive sister, Number 40. Following 40's death 106 would come into her own, proving herself an exceptionally skilled hunter.) The General knew how much we needed collars on this group, and there was an edge of excitement in his voice that left the rest of us amped up and ready to go.

When we arrived Roger had us set the copter down and wait. Since his earlier radio transmission the wolves had moved into a herd of elk—were chasing them, trying to make a kill. He was having trouble sorting things out, didn't know how to direct us what with wolves and elk running every which way. When we finally headed in we discovered the wolves hadn't actually made a kill, that the elk had run off; this was a bit of a relief, given that we try to avoid ever running elk with the helicopter. With the General cruising high above in the Super Cub, barking out landmarks to guide us in, we quickly spotted six members of the pack against the snow. Gary picked out a big gray, got me in for a good shot and we had our first wolf. In quick succession he maneuvered in on another gray, and once again we hit pay dirt. Off in the distance we saw a black wolf running away and we decided to go after it.

I knew this wolf, Number 353, the only black member of the group—a small female that had been with the pack for about a year. Females, by the way, tend to be fast runners, much faster than males, not only because they're somewhat smaller and therefore more agile— traits that make them great hunters—but also because they tend not to hesitate. Males by contrast seem more tuned in to defending territory, rather like a male lion who only looks after ground and leaves the hunting to the females. During darting operations there are times when males will actually turn and look at the oncoming helicopter, ready to take it on if need be, or at least think about taking it on, which tends to give us the split-second advantage we need to dart them.

This little black female had turned on the jets, wasting no time running for broken, rocky country across a mere couple inches of snow. Despite the low probability of capture we flew along with her, just in case she made a mistake. Which is just what happened. Despite having beat us to the punch at the last minute she dove underneath a boulder the size of a small house. At first I thought that was it, we were finished, but then I heard Gary say "We got her," and next thing I knew he was scouting out a place to land. "She's in a hole," he explained. "Go in and see if you can dart her from the ground." A minute later I hopped out of the helicopter, while Gary took off again to transport the two wolves we'd already darted back to the handling crew, to begin processing and collaring.

When I walked up to the rock and looked down into that hole all I could see were the wolf's eyes, blinking at me out of the blackness. There was a light snow falling. To avoid unnecessary injury it's important not to dart an animal from too close, so I had to back up some fifty feet up a slight hill. All the while those blinking eyes were on me, staring intently, though she made no attempt to run for it. I was back as far as I could be to still keep her in my sights, but even at that distance I wanted to make doubly sure my shot placement was perfect, hitting her in a fleshy part of her hindquarter. Yet all I had to go on was the shine of her eyes. I pulled the dart rifle up to my shoulder and aimed to the right about the distance I thought her rear would be from her face. She lay there with her eyes fixed on me while I held the rifle with my finger on the trigger, the two of us locked for several moments in a mutual gaze. I squeezed the trigger and "FSSSSST"—out came the dart. She did nothing. There was no acknowledgment that I'd hit her. I couldn't shoot another dart, not wanting to chance giving her a double dose of tranquilizer, though I also wasn't keen on crawling into the hole to confirm that the first shot had hit the mark. My only option seemed to be to sit in that lightly falling snow, waiting a little while longer before reaching down the hole to grab her foot, which would tell me if she was really out. In the end, though, it proved easier than all that. As I sat and watched I noticed the shine of her eyes slowly disappear, the steady gaze and blinking finally fading to black, signaling that she was indeed asleep.

Even so, when the helicopter landed with project biologist Dan Stahler I wanted to have a backup plan, on the off chance she wasn't drugged after all. I told Dan I was going to load another dart, then stand with the rifle pointed in the direction I figured she would run. Dan, on the other hand, would be the lucky guy to crawl into the hole to fetch her. To be on the safe side he lightly poked her with a long stick, looking for a response. Nothing. Next he crawled down and grabbed her leg lightly, again waiting for a response, getting none. Once we were both comfortable that she was indeed sedated, he went in and grabbed her, carefully passing her out to me. Number 353 was safe in hand.

Capturing this little female was a lucky break. Her behavior was unique among wolves, and that fact meant new opportunities for us to learn. For one thing, she had a habit of splitting off from the pack for long periods, up to a month at a time, traveling alone. Every time we thought she was going to leave for good, dispersing from the group, she always came back. In April of 2004 she had a litter of pups at the same time as the alpha female, Number 106. While the birth of that litter eased her wandering ways somewhat—wolves almost never abandon their pups—still she managed to eke out a fair amount of alone time. It's been nearly a year since we collared her, and only time will tell what this independent little female will do.

An important facet of wolf behavior to keep in mind during darting is that if we manage to catch the alpha female first the alpha male will hang around. The opposite, though, isn't true. Catch the adult male first and the alpha female will make tracks, not waiting to see what happens next. I was reminded of this in February 2004, when moving in to catch wolves of the Cougar Creek Pack near West Yellowstone, Montana. We flew in low, crossing over lands burned in the 1988 fires, the timber regenerating as "dog hair" lodgepole pine—so named because it grows thick, like the hair on a dog's back. We could see the wolves running through the ten- to fifteen-foot-high trees, but branches in the way left us unable to get a shot. At the same time we had to deal with "sucker poles," which are remnant trees from the burn sticking well above the sea of young timber, preventing us from getting low enough in the helicopter for a good shot. Pilot Gary Brennan has a special hatred for sucker poles, and was constantly on the lookout for them—a great priority, since a single strike would bring us down.

As the pursuit unfolded we spotted all but two of the pack of ten wolves spilling into a gully, headed for what we call Dry Fork of Cougar Creek. The two that split off, meanwhile, consisted of a small lead wolf being trailed by a much larger one, undoubtedly a male. No matter what we did, the male simply wouldn't leave her side. Given that February is wolf breeding season in Yellowstone, we quickly surmised that this had to be the alpha pair, so we peeled off from the main group and went in for a closer look. Sure enough, they were both collared. The alpha female, Wolf 151, had first been collared in 1999 while a pup in the Leopold Pack; given that the batteries in these collars last anywhere from three to five years, hers were almost certain to fail any day. Getting our hands on her and replacing that collar would mean that in all likelihood we'd be able to gather data for her entire life, birth to death—an incredibly rare opportunity for any scientific study. I wasted no time letting Gary know through the voice-activated microphone that this smaller wolf was the one I wanted, and wanted badly. "That's our girl!" I shouted. True to form, at that second Gary Brennan—always up for a challenge—came into his own, calling from a virtual treasure of helicopter experience dating all the way back to the Gulf War. His attention firmly fixed on the female now lunging through deep snow, Gary threaded a safe route for me to stick a dart neatly into her butt, in a single shot.

In all honesty, as thrilling as such moments are, I tend to enjoy the aftermath of captured wolves more than the darting itself. Though I actually studied and watched wolves for twenty years before I ever darted one, seeing this side of the animal has been completely new, and highly revealing. Their beauty alone, which reveals itself well at such close quarters, is to me nothing short of remarkable. Through handling a scientist has a chance to become intimately familiar with what he's studying, able to learn in a much more intuitive fashion. There are other advantages too, in that we can gather biological samples, including blood, allowing us to assess not only the condition of the wolf, including its exposure to diseases, but also track its genetic history through DNA. At every such opportunity we also age, weigh, and take physical measurements.

Once darted a wolf typically succumbs to the drug within five minutes. In addition to being the gunner it's my job to gather the sedated animals for the handling crew, which can be physically demanding. Carrying a 120- or 130-pound wolf through two-and-a-half feet of snow, traipsing through tangled woods and steep gullies to a waiting helicopter, is more than enough to wear a body out. In January 2004, for example, we were flying near McBride Lake and darting a 125-pound male wolf from the Slough Creek Pack. Unfortunately he went down in deep woods on a steep grade of some sixty degrees, where no helicopter could possibly land. The pilot, fully aware that this wouldn't be an easy job, dropped me off and headed out to pick up the handling crew.

In the forefront of my mind, on that day and many others, was the fact that I've had back trouble since junior high school. For several weeks during the previous year I'd been barely able to stand up straight or even sit in a chair, having thrown my back out merely by picking up my eighty-five-pound dog after cancer surgery to load her into the back of our car. Indeed, in 2003 the pain was so bad that I'd had to dart with a brace. And though by the time we got to McBride Lake on that January day in 2004 such pain was long gone, the memory of it lingered, needling me as I headed down the hill to pick up what was by any standard an enormous wolf.

Arriving on the scene, it was even worse than I feared. First I attempted the tried-and-true method of hefting him over my shoulders, but that proved impossible; I simply couldn't get him over my head, and each try ended with me on the ground. Next I tried carrying him in my arms but kept slipping backward on the snow-covered slope. I was starting to think there was no way I'd ever get this wolf out by myself, so I began entertaining the idea of calling on the radio for help. Mustering the energy for one more good try, I began crawling up the hill on a contour, holding the wolf by the scruff of the neck and dragging him behind me. Every grunt-filled pull resulted in only a few feet of progress, and it didn't take long before I was winded. Several times I almost lost the poor creature down the steep, snow-covered slope but I held on, terrified by the prospect of having to start over.

After about twenty minutes of this Herculean struggle the helicopter landed again to pick me up. The pilot can't help at all in such situations, being required to stay at all times with the aircraft, which essentially meant that I now had an audience. The pilot signaled me to take my time, so I toiled on, logging at least another ten minutes dragging the wolf in tiny increments, foot by foot, toward the waiting helicopter. By the time I made it I was more than dog tired. The bad news was that this was among the first wolves of the day; there would be others, and I'd have to pull it together in order to be capable of darting more. In fact no sooner had we unloaded the first wolf when Roger Stradley's voice crackled urgently over the radio from the spotter plane, saying "Let's go, let's go, let's go," which of course meant he had other wolves in his sights. A deep breath or two for me, then it was back to the chopper to strap myself in. As pilot Gary Brennan likes to say, when all the stars line up you gotta work, and the stars were definitely lined up: good weather, wolves in the open. And work we did, right up to the edge of dark, catching seven more animals before finally calling it a day.

One last contender for the most memorable day of darting occurred on January 17, 2005—and not just because it was only the second time we'd managed to capture ten wolves before the sun went down. At one point we were pushing hard to catch up with an enormous member of the Agate Creek Pack, male 295 (son of wolf 113, pictured on page 1 of the photo insert). Having been collared before, he was familiar with the drill. And while the last time he saw darters coming toward him he hustled away, this time he was determined to try a different tactic. Suddenly, with the helicopter almost upon him, he turned, considered the situation for a couple of seconds, then bared his teeth and took several steps right toward us. Snow was flying all around, churned by the wash of the helicopter blades. But there he was, fierce in the midst of the uproar, so close the pilot actually had to peel back. For a second I wasn't sure if I'd have to kick him away. (One of the first rules of darting, by the way, is to never shoot an animal turned toward the gun, since it could result in a dart hitting him in the face or penetrating the rib cage.) All in all the encounter left me breathless, inspired by what was a supreme act of defiance.

◆ ◆ ◆

RADIO TRACKING ANIMALS has become a clear staple of professional wildlife biology. Each animal is assigned a unique radio frequency, thereby enabling us to study not just group dynamics, but also individual behavior. For example, when we want to find the alpha male of the Druid Peak Pack we tune the receiver to his specific frequency, listening for the beeps coming from the transmitter around his neck. This region actually played a key role in the development and first use of radio collars; noted biologists Frank and John Craighead, who studied grizzly bears in Yellowstone extensively during the 1960s, were among the first to use them in the wild.[12] Meanwhile in Minnesota, Dave Mech was heavily involved with the design and testing of collars that would ultimately be used on wolves.[13]

Until recently, while collars grew smaller and more reliable, as well as easier to attach and more durable, there'd been relatively little change to the technology. Radio tracking always required biologists to be out in the field, close to his or her subject. Today, however, there's a new collar that allows "office biology" to an extent never known before. These GPS or "global positioning system" collars actually communicate with a satellite, precisely identifying on a grid system where a wolf is located at any given time. This information is then stored in the collar itself, awaiting retrieval. (Some new collars allow downloading electronically before actual retrieval.) Using this kind of technology it's possible for a biologist to program a collar to locate a wolf at virtually any hour of the day or night. While conventional collars are limited to how often we actually locate the wolf, typically once a day, a GPS collar can offer up to forty times that rate. Indeed, systems are just now coming online that will allow tracking of animals in real time, right from your desk. This would allow us to investigate certain events in a timely manner, gaining much more insight into where the wolf went and what it was doing.

A good example of how this technology can be applied involves summer predation rates—in other words, what and how often wolves eat in the warm months. As mentioned earlier, during this season wolves are harder to spot—both because they've broken up into smaller hunting groups, but also because those groups are focused on smaller prey, which in turn makes kill sites harder to detect. Such problems can be solved at least in part with GPS collars, since they allow locations to be determined without anyone actually being there. During the summer of 2004 we fitted two wolves in two different packs with GPS collars—a yearling male from the Geode Creek and a yearling female from Druid Peak—each device programmed to locate the wolves forty times each day. While we actually placed the collar in January, we were able to program it to not begin establishing those locations until May and June, thereby saving battery power in the intervening months. When the summer study period was over we could send a signal to the collar causing it to detach from the wolf. Once detached we were then able to track the signal and retrieve the collar, at which point we could download any remaining data. (Or at least that was the way it was supposed to go. Unfortunately on this one, unbeknownst to us, we ended up providing the manufacturer with some much-needed field-testing.)

Our basic plan was to download locations every week and then hike to "clusters" of established points on the ground to see what was there—why the wolf may have been spending time in that particular location. But we didn't yet know how to calibrate our searches. In other words, would two hours at one spot constitute a kill, or would that event typically require more than two hours? As time went on it became obvious that we'd have to examine many different clusters before we could get a decent feel for how long a wolf spent at any given site, understanding that taking an elk calf requires a lot less time than does a bull elk.

Unfortunately, the yearling female from the Druid Peak Pack we'd chosen for the study ended up being bred that year. This meant our predation study was a bust for this wolf, since rearing pups meant she'd be forgoing hunting activity, instead staying close to the den for a good six weeks after giving birth. This reduced our project to a single male, a two-year-old in the Geode Creek Pack. Happily, his pack's territory was more accessible to us than that of Druid Peak, which made hiking to all these "clusters" a much more reasonable proposition. More importantly, the Geode Creek Pack wasn't all that large. A big pack would mean many small hunting groups, and to get an accurate picture of what the pack was doing all units would have to be tracked. But Geode Creek's smaller size, just six animals, meant the pack would splinter into fewer hunting groups, which in turn meant that the one individual we'd collared would better represent what the entire pack was doing. Indeed, most of the time there was probably only one hunting unit, given that two of the members were breeding females, who wouldn't be hunting much in early summer. That left only four to account for, and on a few occasions we observed them all hunting together.

Through May and June the collar worked like a charm. Dan Stahler, the project biologist leading the study, downloaded from it every week, plotted clusters on the computer, then hiked to each place where the wolf had spent more than two hours. This was an amazing effort, and Matt Metz, Janice Stroud, and Katie Yale worked almost nonstop to help pull if off, while Emily Almberg helped out when she wasn't monitoring both wolves and people in Lamar Valley. What we learned is that wolves do in fact eat less in summer, just as many researchers had hypothesized. The frequency of their kills dropped by about 25 percent compared to winter. Furthermore, and contrary to what many had supposed, wolf predation did not switch exclusively to elk calves, but rather calves were taken only as the opportunity presented itself. This alone was a valuable finding, given that some people had been suggesting wolves were all but wiping out elk calves soon after they were born.

We've currently got plans in the works to extend our use of GPS technology, using it to ask ever more detailed questions. One of these involves wolf interactions with other carnivores, including black bears, grizzly bears, and cougars. Working closely with other researchers we hope to fit all four big carnivores with satellite collars and program them to the same schedule. We could thus discover how the different species interact—how the landscape is divided up, who's dominating who. GPS collars will also help us refine our wolf pack territory maps, greatly enhancing our understanding of where they actually go.

There are, it should be said, some drawbacks to this technology. For one thing, while a conventional collar costs roughly $300, a GPS collar is currently more than ten times that amount. What's more, GPS technology draws far more heavily on battery power, making the collars last only about ten to twelve months, compared to three to five years with a conventional system. Though performance will no doubt improve with time, for now this is a serious liability, given how difficult, expensive, and invasive it is to catch every single wolf. There's another limitation to GPS as well, and it has to do with the fact that the biologist no longer sees the animals being tracked. Without a visual connection it's impossible to know how many other wolves an individual animal is with, let alone whether it might be interacting with an elk, coyote, or grizzly bear. While GPS data might show up as a cluster, suggesting a kill, there's no guarantee that's what's going on, nor is there any hint of the kind of prey animal that's been taken—be it cow, bull or calf elk, or even bison. Given such drawbacks, it seems unlikely that GPS systems will ever entirely replace tracking with more conventional collars.

◆ ◆ ◆

ALL THIS TALK of research brings to mind what's become a common dispute in some circles about the practice of science, versus that of natural history. From a historical perspective, of course, all early science began with natural history. It was widely understood that before any scientific questions could be asked it was necessary to have a thorough understanding of the habits and characteristics of your subject. But in recent years some have been critical of such approaches, concerned that the observation part of the equation could well overshadow critical thinking. Seen through the lens of that concern a man like Adolph Murie might be seen as "merely" a natural historian, since much of what he did was to go far afield in Mt. McKinley National Park and watch wolves.

But Ade, as he was affectionately known, spent countless hours so engaged, in the process witnessing not just wildlife, but wild relationships of all kinds. His widow, Louise Murie McLeod, describes his labor-intensive approach to wildlife watching as "the Adolph Murie way." (She sometimes went on to describe his dedication with a measure of exasperation. "He turned down trips to Africa so he could go back to Alaska. One would have thought twenty-five summers was enough.") Murie's style—patient, slow, noting his observations in a journal instead of on a spreadsheet—is today largely out of vogue. Most modern researchers specialize on tightly focused topics, always on the lookout for short-term results—an approach driven in large part by the institutions that provide grant money for the work, as well as the all-important opportunities for publishing. Yet no matter how much we try to push things, answers to the really big questions reveal themselves very slowly. Wolves in particular have been highly circumspect when it comes to showing their hand—proving to be an animal of secrets, living in ecosystems still replete with mysteries. The wolf-moose study on Isle Royale, which is the longest running carnivore research of its kind in the world, came up with different answers about wolf-moose dynamics in every decade of the study. In other words, the answers coming from Isle Royale depended entirely on which decade you happened to be in when you asked the question.[14]

Modern science rests on an insistence that a researcher ask a specific question. Beyond that, some sort of manipulation should be applied—either to the subject or the habitat—preferably with a control site in place. The ultimate ideal would be manipulation with random replication, which means testing your manipulation at more than one site—each of those sites assigned randomly—and at the same time having a control site where nothing is manipulated at all. From a purely scientific perspective, the mainstay of our research here in Yellowstone—using radio collars to track wolves—might be considered only a modest improvement over the kind of plain observation Adolph Murie was so famous for. Yet while this current formula for good science—a mix of manipulation and replication and control sites—make for a worthy goal, it's nearly impossible to do things this way here in Yellowstone, given that we're talking about wolf-prey systems that span thousands of square miles. Besides, in order to secure what would be considered an adequate sample size we'd need a lot more wolves than we currently have, or will ever have. In short, though we aspire to conduct the strongest science possible here in Yellowstone, we'll likely always fall somewhat short.

While doing our best to meet modern scientific protocols, I feel it's also worth recalling what's best about natural history: going out into the environment and obtaining direct experience through observation, then drawing conclusions from what you see. In that sense we're trying to be both scientists *and* naturalists—embracing not just our best researchers, but also those men and women living in the stream of people like John Burroughs and John Muir. Population dynamics matter. But then so do individual narratives. For this reason we'll continue to work hard to keep the Yellowstone wolf reintroduction effort a field-based program, making certain that work plans and ideas flow from the ground up, rather than from the office down.

CHAPTER 9

THE VIEW FROM
TEN YEARS OUT

The wolves of Yellowstone are home again, having
resurrected the old haunts of long ago, living out their
lives in this wild country much as other generations of wolves
had done before them. Only time will tell, of course, but I believe the

ten-year mark finds us at the close of what can be thought of as the first of three phases of wolf recovery. This first decade has been all about growth—a time when the wolves used every trick in the book (and a few not in the book) to take advantage of open territory and a tremendous prey base. Individual animals, both adults and pups, have been big and healthy. Dispersal was low, with some wolves choosing to stay in their natal packs for four or even five years—something rarely seen elsewhere in North America. A number of packs enjoyed multiple litters.

Yet the end of 2004 finds the wolf population the same or even slightly lower than it was the year before—the first time such a decline has happened other than in 1999–2000, when, as previously mentioned, we think a disease called parvovirus hit the pups. By all appearances we're crossing a bridge that will lead to the second phase of this reintroduction—an era marked by a reduction in the weights of both adults and pups living on the northern range, more often than not a precursor to declining survival rates. More wolves will disperse from their families. Conflict among the packs will increase, especially on the northern range where even now the territories are tightly packed, resulting in more animals dying in skirmishes.

Finally there will come to the Yellowstone wolf population a third, more long-term phase. During the early portion of this period we may see continued declines in both the numbers of wolves and elk, but this will be followed by a time when both predator and prey reach a kind of equilibrium with their surrounding environment. As the number of wolves go down, meaning there's more food to go around, the rate of dispersal by young wolves will once again settle at modest levels. So too then will there be fewer conflicts between the packs. Of course this entire scenario is subject to a host of wild cards—events that can serve to reset the game, if you will—from massive wildfires like those that occurred in 1988, to a host of diseases ranging from parvovirus, to mange, to distemper.

With the end of this first phase of the wolf cycle, the time has come to remove these animals from the endangered species list. Delisting is, after all, an indication that there are enough wolves in the system to allow more flexible management options—which could potentially include recreational harvests outside the park—without endangering the population. From a biological standpoint, this is unquestionably the case. That said, the plan under which wolves were reintroduced calls for Montana, Idaho, and Wyoming to take over management of the species after federal managers achieve restoration, so long as each state has a solid plan for protecting the population in the years to come. Idaho and Montana have been sitting on approved plans for some time. Wyoming's strategy, however, is to basically treat wolves as predators outside a very limited area, thereby opening them to being shot on sight—a proposal the U.S. Fish and Wildlife Service (the agency responsible for managing endangered species) has found unacceptable. Rather than revise their management proposal so it passes muster the state has chosen to sue the government, thereby tying up the delisting process in the courts. It's interesting to note that the original plan for this reintroduction, seldom talked about, was to have the U.S. Fish and Wildlife Service actually reintroduce the wolves, with the states managing them from the very beginning. The states vetoed this idea, sensing that wolves were way too much of a political hot potato.

Not that Wyoming's lawsuit will be the only legal action. At this point it seems certain that some in the environmental community will move to prevent delisting, either because they don't want to see wolves hunted, or in some cases because they don't believe the animal can withstand lower levels of protection. As Mike Phillips put it, though, "It's important to be reasonable. With a system like Yellowstone in place the gray wolf can withstand a great deal of human exploitation and still thrive. They'll continue to be wild. And they'll continue to inspire." What's potentially going to be lost in the fight against delisting is a fantastic opportunity for the American public to see this project as evidence that the Endangered Species Act really works. Given that the act is often under fierce attack—some would say its very existence is now threatened—it seems vital to show the nation what is in truth an outstanding success. As John Varley points out, "What this reintroduction may show is that we *can* restore ecosystems to some semblance of what they were before European settlement. And more important still, that we can live with them."

I recall one of my professors in graduate school making the comment that the worst thing that can happen to wildlife biology is for it to end up in the courts. By and large lawsuits don't help the wolves of Yellowstone. What's more, land management and political leaders in other parts of the country who might otherwise accept this predator know full well that getting a wolf population means legal action, and for that reason alone they tend to do everything possible to avoid any talk of reintroductions. Were there a way to resolve problems more reasonably without falling into the quagmire of the court system, wolves might well be able to be successfully placed elsewhere in years to come. But it would require a coming together of those genuinely willing to seek solutions, refusing to let the process be hijacked by people on both sides who show up primarily to thump their chests and draw lines in the sand. Likewise the wildlife management agency involved must be fully present, completely supportive, with neither hidden agendas nor backroom deals.[1]

In addition to struggles over delisting, there also remains today a considerable bone of contention for some residents living near greater Yellowstone—one unlikely to disappear anytime soon—having to do with wolves and livestock. On one hand such concerns are well placed, as over the past decade wolves have certainly been guilty on numerous occasions of killing sheep, cattle, horses, and dogs. If there's any good news to report, it's that wolves have killed considerably fewer domestic animals than was originally predicted in the Environmental Impact

Statement, which estimated a population of a hundred wolves in Yellowstone would each year cause the deaths of between 38 and 110 sheep, and from 3 to 37 cows. Livestock death from other causes, from weather to wild dogs, continues to outpace wolf kills by a staggering margin.

Of course that's little comfort if you happen to be the unfortunate rancher staring at the remains of a cow or sheep recently devoured by a pack of wolves. Thanks in large part to the tireless work of Hank Fischer, near the beginning of the reintroduction the national conservation group Defenders of Wildlife set up a fund to compensate ranchers for wolf-related livestock losses. Sadly, Defenders would be the only major environmental group in America willing to not only acknowledge the potential damage that wolves bring, but actually spend down their own bank account trying to ease it. By and large wolf supporters and detractors alike have preferred to stay on their own sides of the fence, happy to hurl stones at one another. Admittedly, this has been a wonderful tool for attracting new funds and new members. But such positions have led not only to more livestock being lost than necessary, but more wolves, as well.

Even with such a compensation program in place, some ranchers claim—and there's research to support their view—that for every animal known to have been killed by wolves there are others taken for which no evidence is ever found.[2] What's more, a number of producers have told me that despite not having lost any cows, their cattle tend to weigh in less at the end of the grazing season from having been stressed by wolves. And finally, no one can argue that going to all the trouble to prevent wolf kills requires time and energy that could be more profitably spent doing lots of other chores from a never-ending list of things one has to do to run a ranch.

Without question, what's been most successful so far in addressing wolf-livestock conflicts are efforts focused on prevention, which typically means providing some sort of deterrent out in the field with the sheep or cattle. In one vivid example a rancher who had wolves close by (the pack had actually located their summer rendezvous site adjacent to his cows) decided to ride the herd daily. While the wolves did chase his cows a few times, none were ever taken. Meanwhile a neighboring rancher several miles away rode his herd only once a week, and ended up suffering a loss. In a sense we need to lean on some basic management principles long used in other places, including parts of Europe, where a combination of shepherds and multiple guard dogs has all but eliminated predator kills. A recently launched program of the Predator Conservation Alliance in Bozeman, Montana, now provides volunteers to literally baby-sit cattle during the critical calving season, thereby deterring wolves. Again, the vast majority of wolves simply don't recognize sheep or cows as a potential food source. The trick is to discourage those few mavericks tempted to give them a try.

Though there aren't any domestic sheep or cattle grazing in Yellowstone National Park, the backcountry is nonetheless rich with horse traffic, summer to fall. The vast majority of outfitters continue to let their horses run loose at night, and few have had any trouble with wolves. During summer months I routinely do fieldwork by horseback, riding and camping in some of the highest density wolf areas in Yellowstone, and have yet to encounter a problem. Not everyone, though, can make that claim. Retired park ranger Gerald Mernin had Mollie's Pack move in on his horses one night, harassing them just outside his flashlight beam for a good couple of hours before finally retreating. Mernin and ranger Patty Bean did about the only thing they could do, which was to sit up with the horses, placing themselves between their stock and the wolves. (Just because I haven't had any such problems in the backcountry doesn't mean I sleep all that well. Most nights I lie awake listening for the horse bells, jumping up at the slightest indication of a problem. As Ed Bangs likes to say, "Life with wolves is never easier, but it's always more interesting.") Though as yet there are no studies to prove it, I've come to believe the liberal use of bells is helpful, as is mixing in mules with horses. Mules have a well-earned reputation for being bold and cantankerous toward wolves, often perfectly willing to approach them, which tends to send the wolves hightailing off to less disputed ground.

While wolf-livestock problems can certainly be moderated, there's probably no way to stop them entirely. In the summer of 2003, several wolves were chasing horses around in Gardner's Hole—perhaps in part because earlier in the summer a dead horse had been left out for them to eat. I ended up being the lucky one given the assignment of "solving" the situation, so I called Dave Mech for advice. Mech, who tends to have insightful answers to about any wolf question imaginable, this time had no remedies. "If that problem had a solution," he said, "we would've implemented it thirty years ago."

◆ ◆ ◆

AFTER A DECADE of hard work, carried out not just by some outstanding professionals and volunteers, but in large part by the wolves themselves, it's worth taking a look at what a fully restored Yellowstone wolf population looks like. As we mentioned earlier, the diversity of conditions in the national park—the drier, prey-abundant lands of the northern range, offering one of the highest prey concentrations in the world, versus slimmer pickings in the park's interior—makes for a rich and varied portrait.

As of 2005 there were seven wolf packs living on the northern range: Swan Lake (formed in 2000), Leopold (formed in 1996 and named after the famous Aldo Leopold), Geode Creek (2002), Slough Creek (2003), Agate Creek (2002), Druid Peak (1996), and one other new pack called Specimen Ridge, formed in 2004 but now gone from our radar. Because they all live on the northern range each of these groups are similar when it comes to the size of their territories, what they eat, how many pups they have, and how big the packs are. Even survival rates and other important demographic and ecological aspects are comparable.

Again, the bounty of prey on the northern range makes it a highly desirable location, tightening territories and igniting some forceful interactions. Indeed, if anything can be said to have marked the months leading up to the ten year anniversary of the reintroduction, it would be a widespread state of unrest and turmoil. As of this writing, for example, the Slough Creek Pack has grown to fourteen animals—twice the size of the Druid Peak group. With all the bluster and might such numbers afford, the Slough Creek wolves have rolled into the Lamar Valley, pushing the legendary Druids eastward, driving them to the very margins of the territory they held with such ferocity for more than eight years.

Once we drift southward through Yellowstone we find greater snowfall, as well as striking differences in the number of thermal features—favorite hangouts for prey animals through the bitterly cold months of winter. Each wolf pack has adapted to these variables in its own way, meaning that each is somewhat unique in how it lives. Mollie's Pack, for instance (remember, these wolves were originally called the Crystal Creek Pack and were the first to live in Yellowstone's famed Lamar Valley), now lives primarily in Pelican Valley. While offering tremendous summer habitat for elk, bison, and deer, in winter the valley turns extremely harsh, bereft of deer and most elk, with only a hardy bunch of about two hundred bison staying on. While occasionally Mollie's wolves find an elk wintering near one of the many thermal springs in the area, especially around Astringent Creek, these tend to be bulls—not exactly easy prey, even for a pack of wolves. Prior to that time when bison have been weakened by winter the wolves in the interior of the park will travel far and wide searching for elk. Perhaps in part due to these tough conditions (as well as the fact that grizzlies often steal their kills), Mollie's Pack has twice been through cycles where their pack was very large, only to be followed by a crash. As mentioned earlier, in 2000 the pack was down to just four animals and failed to reproduce, which is highly unusual.

The tale of Mollie's wolves has recently grown still more remarkable. In the third week of December 2004, on a routine overflight we found dead from unknown causes the alpha female of the pack, Number 174—her body lying in a remote location southeast of the Pelican Valley, near Jones Pass. Strangely, the day after discovering her body we failed to find a single other member of the pack. We've still not found them. Our sense that something odd was afoot took on new weight at the point we flew over the group's traditional home ground in Pelican Valley, where scavangers from coyotes to ravens to bald eagles were feeding on a dead bison. But not a wolf in sight—as far as we know, the first time Mollie's pack ever failed to descend on a winter carcass. Some of us are quietly wondering if this dynamic, forceful pack, having for so long prevailed against the rugged conditions of central Yellowstone, with the loss of their leader has simply disintegrated. If so, I'd be awfully curious to know if their demise had anything to do with routinely losing carcasses to bears.

Not too far from Pelican Valley is the Nez Perce Pack, formed in 1998, whose territory embraces the Madison-Firehole river drainages. Subsisting on the smallest elk herd in the park, roughly five hundred animals,[3] these wolves too have had to learn how to kill bison, each year managing to take more of them as the elk herd slowly declines.[4] Unlike Mollie's Pack, where bison only number a couple hundred, the Nez Perce Pack has access to several thousand animals of the Great Central herd. As wolves have done through eons the Nez Perce Pack is adapting, learning how to kill what is arguably the most formidable prey animal in the park. Like Mollie's Pack, thermal features in the area play an important part in their day-to-day lives. (Curiously, in late 2004 the Nez Perce pack, so constant in their territory over the past seven years, have been seen for several weeks at a variety of sites on the northern range, including Hellroaring, Specimen Ridge, Mount Everts, and Junction Butte. Meanwhile the Biscuit Basin Pack has been traveling through all the nooks and crannies that Nez Perce used to call home.)

Near the Nez Perce Pack are a few newer, and thus lesser known packs: one in the Gibbon River area, as well as a breeding pair called the Biscuit Basin Pack south of Old Faithful, hanging on in what seems questionable habitat. Meanwhile, we were surprised to find living in the Cougar Creek area the Cougar Creek Pack, formed in 2000, made up of animals from the Leopold group of the northern range, as well as what we think are unmarked wolves from the Nez Perce Pack. I would've thought Cougar Creek to be simply too inhospitable. While the areas lie along the main path bison use to leave Yellowstone in hard winters, there are never large numbers of elk here. Like the Nez Perce Pack the Cougar Creek wolves subsist on a combination of elk and bison, growing ever more efficient at taking the latter. Unique to this pack is an abundant beaver population. While Yellowstone overall isn't prime beaver habitat, one of the main hubs for this animal does lie within Cougar Creek wolf territory. Cougar, Gneiss, Maple, Campanula, and Duck creeks all have beaver colonies, as does the Madison River, each drainage thus providing wolves a significant food source throughout the summer. (Beavers only reach high numbers in three areas of Yellowstone National Park—the Cougar Creek region, the Yellowstone Delta, and the Bechler River. Not surprisingly, all three have wolf packs.)

Moving north again from the Cougar Creek Pack is the Chief Joseph Pack, formed in 1996. Early on in the reintroduction these animals resided mostly within Yellowstone National Park, though in the last few years they've been ranging outside in the state of Montana, confining their park time mostly to denning activity. Their territory embraces the only highway thoroughfare in the park, State Road 191, and as a result this pack has suffered more vehicle mortality than any other group. As there are virtually no bison here elk is their primary prey, along with an occasional meal of beaver. These wolves have an enormous territory, suggesting they need to travel widely in order to keep themselves fed. Occasionally they manage to run afoul of humans by killing livestock. As a result, a few have been killed through control actions outside the park.

Jumping to the southern boundary we find two other packs, the dynamics of which are again quite different. First is the Yellowstone Delta Pack—formed in 1995 as the Soda Butte Pack, but later moved to the Yellowstone River Delta on the southeast arm of Yellowstone Lake. This pack has the distinction of living in the most remote spot in the contiguous forty-eight United States. Much like the territory of Mollie's Pack, prey abounds here in the summer, with plenty of elk, moose, and deer, even an occasional lone bison. And also like Mollie's Pack, the vast majority of these animals vacate the area in winter, leaving behind mostly moose and a few rogue bison. That in turn triggers big movements in the pack. Most of these are journeys to lands outside Yellowstone National Park on the adjacent Bridger-Teton Wilderness, but now and then the animals end up drifting to places that lie beyond our ability to track. Yet every year, much like the Chief Joseph Pack, they settle back down on park lands to den and raise their pups. While the Delta wolves have no thermal features to hold wintering prey, like the Cougar Creek Pack they do enjoy an abundant supply of beavers.

One other characteristic of the Delta wolves worth mentioning is their fascinating, if annoying habit of removing their radio collars. As one might almost expect, it would fall to the most remote pack in the park—and therefore the most difficult and expensive to collar—to end up with the strongest hankering to chew off the hardware. Not able to remove collars on their own they simply sidle up next to pack mates, who seem happy to oblige. One year we collared five wolves in this pack, and within six months every one was chewed off. We finally grew so desperate we had the collars—already a tough blend of steel cord and fiberglass—fitted with brass studs. These too they removed with little difficulty. For a couple years we only had one collared wolf in this pack, the alpha female, who given her dominant role would be unlikely to let a pack mate nuzzle up and gnaw away at her collar. Though this chewing habit has been seen in only a few packs, once wolves learn the technique it remains a problem forevermore. I sometimes wonder if the day will come when the Delta wolves will just plain give us the slip for good.

Finally is the Bechler Pack, formed in 2002. This is another group living in what I would've considered less than ideal wolf habitat. The pack was formed when a very large male from the Rose Creek wolves—now strikingly white, unmistakable from an aircraft—dispersed to start a new pack in the southwest corner of the park. Their success so far may be due to having enjoyed mild winters almost from the time they moved in, which has allowed a smattering of elk and moose to hang around in the cold months. In a normal winter, though, the Bechler is devoid of virtually all prey. Unlike certain other harsh places we've mentioned, here the snow typically gets so deep no ungulates can survive. Even with the recent mild winters this pack still tends to leave now and then, traveling widely through the Targhee National Forest in search of prey. A return to more normal climate conditions will almost certainly make life tougher for them, possibly causing the group to journey even farther afield. This penchant for traveling, along with the fact that they're such a long distance from our airport base in Gardiner, means we know less about this pack than any other.

Again, Yellowstone's wolf packs are extraordinarily stable, with few ever dissolving or breaking apart. Indeed, seventeen of the nineteen wolf packs that have formed in Yellowstone since reintroduction are still together—a situation no doubt in part thanks to their having been protected from human exploitation. And yet it's hard to say what the next ten years will bring. We could well be at a population high point, with numbers not growing much larger than what they are right now. Most of the places wolves can survive, after all, have now been settled, and as prey declines wolves will decline with them. One thing seems certain: the stories of the packs, as well as the tales of individual wolves, will be no less fascinating in the second decade of Yellowstone wolf recovery than in the first.

In truth absolutely no one thought this reintroduction would go so well. Certainly the designers of the project deserve credit for preparing the way, reaching out to and informing the public, ultimately giving the wolves a solid structure within which they could thrive. What's more, in addition to an extraordinary group of volunteers there's also been a dedicated team of professional scientists whose company I've been privileged to keep. I began my own tenure in Yellowstone as the project biologist in 1994, taking over as project leader in May of 1997 after a brilliant performance in that slot by the indefatigable Mike Phillips. Slipping in behind me as biologist from 1998 through 2000 was a highly seasoned salt-of-the-cougar world, Kerry Murphy.

After Murph would come "Dano" Dan Stahler, who'd cut his teeth in the wolf world by trapping in Minnesota with Mike Nelson and Dave Mech. Dan first came to Yellowstone to help out with wolf den research, going on to perform superbly on various winter studies. He gained his Master's degree with us through the University of Vermont, working with world-renowned raven researcher Bernd Heinrich examining the relationships between wolves and ravens. Dan's still with us, spearheading our scavenger research, not to mention some fairly complicated tasks associated with GPS collars. Then there was Wayne Brewster, considered one of the main architects of the entire wolf reintroduction (Yellowstone was actually Wayne's third job in twenty years related to wolf recovery in the American West), as well as noted biologist and head of the Yellowstone Center for Resources, John Varley.

Finally, the glue that holds much of this project together is Debra Guernsey—a long-time veteran of the project who quite literally worked her way up through the ranks, starting out as one of the very first volunteers in April of 1995. For sheer tenure she outdistances almost everyone, thereby possessing an indispensable historic view. Right from the beginning Deb gave her all to this effort, as a volunteer sleeping in the office when necessary, on occasion even selling personal possessions to keep doing the work she loved. Whenever there was something to be done she did it, right down to making runs for roadkill and then gutting elk—tasks required to feed the wolves while they were in the acclimation pens. Once on the payroll she eventually settled in to become our database manager and information whiz kid, and at this point it's safe to say that she has a firm grasp on just about everything. She knows what to do, who to call, who needs to know, what to say, who to buy gear from—and in general, what's important and what's not. Doing it all, every day, with grace and style. "I never thought I'd love it this much," says Deb. "Every single day comes a moment when I stop and suddenly feel really, really grateful."

◆ ◆ ◆

THE WOLVES of Yellowstone have done a beautiful job at what they do best—securing and defending territory, raising young, mastering the ebbs and flows of their prey. Along the way they've been teaching all of us—revealing not just their own natural histories, but some basic principles about wolf restoration in general. Today we understand much

better the importance of launching a project like this into a core protected area like Yellowstone, a place containing sufficient quantities of
resources to allow a population to become fully anchored. Indeed, of
the three Northern Rocky Mountain recovery zones that were a part
of this reintroduction—Yellowstone, central Idaho, and northwest
Montana—Yellowstone and Idaho are doing best because they rest on
a foundation of exceptional habitat, places not just devoid of humans
and livestock, but with abundant prey. Northwest Montana, meanwhile, though blessed with large and magnificent areas like the Bob
Marshall Wilderness and Glacier National Park, proved less than ideal
wolf habitat primarily because the elevations are too high to support
year-round prey.

The remarkable success of the Yellowstone Wolf Project likely also
rests in the fact that we started not with zoo-raised animals, but rather
those already familiar with the rigors of living in the wild. Upon release
from their acclimation pens these wolves knew right away what to do,
in some cases killing elk within a few hundred yards of the pen. Through
no fault of their own other projects have had to reintroduce captive-
reared wolves, animals that have to navigate a far steeper, more difficult
learning curve before they at last possess the skills necessary for survival.

Right now we have significantly more wolves in the United States
than we did just two decades ago—not just in the northern Rocky
Mountains, but in the American Southwest, the Lake States of Minnesota, Wisconsin and Michigan, and finally, with another species known
as the red wolf, in North Carolina. Where else might wolf recovery make
sense? One place attractive to many are the long, broad sweeps of forest comprising northern New England. Though most of these lands are
privately owned by paper companies, that fact would hardly trouble
wolves, since healthy populations can certainly be supported in a working forest. Assuming there exists some form of protection from human
exploitation, the same habitats that support whitetail deer and moose

would also support wolves. Some have also argued for restoration of wolves in the southern Rocky Mountains of Colorado and northern New Mexico. Again, there are broad sweeps of public land in this region, though a fair percentage are at high elevations, much like those of northwestern Montana, which influences the availability of prey.

To some degree wolves will by themselves probably expand to areas in eastern Oregon, northern Utah and northern Colorado—all of which have already had animals make it across their borders. Wolf 293 of the Swan Lake Pack was hit on the road near Denver, which even in a straight line—and wolves don't travel in straight lines—is a trip of about four hundred miles. Meanwhile two years ago male wolf 253 of the Druid Peak Pack was captured in a coyote trap not terribly far from Salt Lake City, Utah, then brought back to a release site near Jackson, Wyoming. Having heard reports that 253 was traveling with another wolf at the time of capture—I assumed a female—I boldly predicted (on television, no less) that he would head straight back to the Beehive State. Hardly. Instead he made a beeline for the Lamar Valley, where he's been ever since. Idaho, meanwhile, currently has wolves busting at the seams to swim across the Snake River into Oregon—something they will likely do if they haven't already.

Yet such movements by individual pioneers hardly mean a wolf population will anchor in these places naturally. After all, wolves had been living for decades across the Canadian border near northwest Montana, yet never managed to anchor themselves in greater Yellowstone. Even if unverified sightings of individual animals in and around the national park were correct, never did it result in the species rooting here. Research would suggest that such occasional travelers would be far too isolated, not to mention vulnerable to a major gauntlet of human-caused mortality, to ever establish breeding populations.

The twentieth century saw astonishing changes in the world of wolves. From roughly 1900 to 1950 there was a mantra common even among land managers, declaring the only good wolf to be a dead one. That notion, combined with increasingly efficient technology, led to a brand of wholesale extirpation never before seen anywhere on the continent. The killing fever finally spent, wolves received a break for a time, able to reclaim in the 1960s and 1970s at least some of the ground previously lost—this, until concerns by hunters and livestock producers started the guns firing again, this time mostly from the open doors of helicopters.

In the 1980s and 1990s came recovery—the gray wolf in Michigan and Wisconsin, the red wolf in North Carolina, the Mexican wolf in New Mexico. Then finally here in Yellowstone, some seventy years after the last wolf was killed in the Lamar Valley. Today the world's first national park—some say America's best idea ever—is again feeling the footsteps of wolf packs, again resounding with their soulful howls. In this protected space the wolf will prove himself a survivor extraordinaire, one that will hopefully remain a part of this wonderful web of life for centuries to come. For those of us who've been here watching and listening, it's been one of the most enthralling decades of our lives.

EPILOGUE

OVER THE YEARS I've done interviews about the Yellowstone Wolf Project with reporters from around the world. More often than not, after wading through chewy matters of science and wildlife management and even politics, there comes a request to recount my most memorable experience with wolves. I understand well the need for such a question, the eagerness to catch a glimpse of the drama that comes from working in magnificent settings with one of the most captivating predators on earth. So even though for me there's no such thing as a favorite experience, I do my best to oblige. But when a journalist for the BBC recently asked me this question, what came to mind were different strings of images—ones less dramatic than modest, less filled with adrenaline than awe: a wolf coming to within a few feet of my tent, pausing there before wandering back through the tall grass into the dark of night; being in a canoe in the Arctic, watching a wolf flee on first catching sight of me only to return moments later to the river bank to watch as I drifted past; out in the chill of early morning, when a big male strode out of the fog and looked right through me, then turned and disappeared into the mist.

For whatever reason, during this interview it dawned on me that individual dramas—battles with grizzlies, interpack struggles over territory, even the stirring beauty offered by any of the more than two dozen wolves I touch with my own hands every year—were less important than the simple sense of wonder that had been kindled by even the most fleeting encounters. Held within a wolf's gaze has been everything I've needed to keep alive my sense of connection to the earth. The fact that I live in a time when these sorts of opportunities are increasingly rare has on one hand left me with a profound feeling of gratitude for being able to do the work I do. On the other hand, that very same rarity—the fact that it's become unusual for people to have any sort of regular dose of nature, let alone trading stares with wolves—leaves me acutely aware of how much the culture has lost. Gone from most people's lives are the simple, wondrous prompts of nature, triggers that once sparked in us not just a sense of beauty, but the pleasures of place. Therein sits the weight, the burden of these times. And it lies heavy as a stone in the heart of even the richest life.

◆ ◆ ◆

November 1, 2004. Once again drifting high above Yellowstone, Roger Stradley and I look down onto the same lands that just twelve weeks ago were drunk with green, finding them today hunkered under a heavy layer of snow. The same animals that in August seemed not to have a care in the world appear edgy, anxious. The elk are moving, large groups of a hundred, two hundred amassing on Geode Bench and on the slopes of Hellroaring, others drifting toward winter range in the Lamar Valley.

As elk begin to travel so do the wolves. Given that it's been a couple weeks since I've flown, it takes me a while to figure out where everyone is. The Leopold Pack—now the big cheese of the northern range, after a decade of that honor belonging either to Rose Creek or

Druid Peak—are throwing their weight around, pushing eastward into new territory. Today we find twenty-two out of a pack of at least twenty-four animals. Though our view is blocked by a weave of timber, given all the birds milling about they're probably on a kill. Geode, meanwhile, is pressing the park boundary, while Rose Creek has vanished altogether.

We fly on to the Slough Creek Pack and spot eight of them testing the waters with a couple of bull elk. As the wolves approach the elk merely stand erect, casting a proud, even daring look, at which point the Slough Creek Pack thinks better of it and simply walks away. Thirty minutes later we see the pack again, this time pressing down on a herd of twenty cow elk and calves—running right at them, predators and prey flying downhill in a high-speed chase lasting for a good mile and a half. One wolf in particular seems intensely driven to grab a certain cow elk, but in the end never gets close. The last we see he's all by his lonesome on a snow-covered hill, the breath from his panting rising in the frozen air. We find Agate Creek on the backside of Specimen Ridge, and after that a few animals from Druid Peak scattered across the Lamar Valley. Having recently lost both of their alphas, the once large and glorious Druids are now in a state of disarray.

I'm freezing. As we slide over Mirror Plateau, heading for Pelican Valley, I ask Roger for some warm air, only to learn that the airplane's heater is on the fritz. Far below us, the Pelican Valley is frozen to stillness, as if it were already the dead of winter. Mollie's wolves are down there, gathered around a fallen bull bison. Shadows on the ground, though, make it impossible to see whether there's blood on the snow, leaving us unsure if the animal was taken by the pack or merely died from some other cause. Either way, it's the first time in years we've found a kill in this valley without a grizzly on it. It seems much too early, but maybe the big bears are already tucked in, curled out of sight somewhere in rocky dens, dreaming away the slow roll of winter.

Finally comes the long, sweet cruise down the east side of Yellowstone Lake, searching for the Delta wolves. We never do manage to find them, which is a little strange given that the elk haven't yet completely pulled out of the Thorofare. Gone too are the elk hunters, most having been able to yet again fill their tags. From this great meandering valley we drift west across Two Ocean Plateau, finding the branches of the trees at these higher elevations utterly whitewashed in snow. Nearby the Snake River is sluggish, choked by a thousand chunks of ice. By now the cold has crept not just into my body, but my mind. At one point I catch myself feeling around in my pocket for the keys that would let us into a backcountry cabin on the ground below—thinking that if our plane goes down, our only chance will be to get inside and start a fire.

As it happens the Nez Perce wolves elude us, too, probably off on a foray outside the park looking for elk. The eleven-member Cougar Creek Pack, meanwhile, is in their usual spot, while the Gibbon Meadows wolves have a bull elk down—a cloud of ravens and magpies flitting around the kill. As we make our way back toward Gardiner I listen for the radio signals of a few other missing wolves, hear not a single one. Strangely, back at the airport—situated at lower elevation—it's autumn again, brown and dry. Yet the winter we've been flying through lingers in my bones, the hours spent in the back of the plane having left me cold and numb and with a touch of shiver. Roger sympathizes, says he'll get the heater fixed before the next flight. No matter. I'm thinking that being cold is a small price of admission for this feast of nature—the wolves and the elk, the snow and ice and the frozen mountains, the beautiful emptiness that is Yellowstone at the brink of winter.

VOLUNTEERS

It seems only fitting to honor the great team of volunteers who helped make the Yellowstone wolf recovery such a resounding success. With special thanks for your insights, your dedication, your passion.

Almberg, Emily
Anderson, Carol
Andre, Melissa
Auer, Jessica
Babcock, Isaac
Bean, Jack
Belmonte, Lisa
Bergmann, Eric
Billman, Hilary
Bly-Honness, Kristy
Boone, Daniel
Brecht, Charles
Breck, Stewart
Brewster, Eric
Brooks, Tracy
Brown, Paul
Buchwald, Robert
Bucki, Adam
Campbell, Craig
Cayou, Joe

Chin, Susan
Clack, Karen
Cleere, Erin
Cole, Dana
Davies, Chase
Dawn, Deanna
Eaton, Mitch
Evans, Shaney
Farris, Stephani
Fenty, Brent
Ferguson, Gary
Fitzherbert, Emily
Frame, Paul
Franseco, Fonseca
Geremia, Chris
Gerum, Scott
Good, John
Graf, Dan
Gray, Rachel
Guernsey, Deb

Hallingstad, Eric
Hartsough, Matt
Henry, Will
Hessick, Kristin
Holmquist, Brett
Honness, Kevin
Hudson, Tim
Huntzinger, Brett
Irvin, Cole
Jacobs, Amy
Johnson, Ben
Johnson, Brian
Jones, Jennifer
Koitzsch, Ky
Krevitz, Alex
Laursen, Scott
Lindh, Hilary
Lindsay, Scott
Lineweaver, Deb
Lyons, Macneil

MacNulty, Daniel
Mao, Julie
McIntyre, Rick
Metz, Matt
Miller, Guy
Mills, Gus
Montgomery, Robert
Moore, Jeff
Muller, Chris
Naftal, Stephanie
Nelson, Abby
Nelson, Julia
Passmore, Bruce
Patrick, Nichole
Paul, Kylie
Peer, Melissa
Pils, Andy
Pils, Jennifer

Rathmall, Ray
Redman, Lessie
Robinson, Betsy
Roscrow, Lynne
Sadoo, Tamara
Saunders, Melissa
Schaefer, Carrie
Schlickeisen, Derek
Smith, J. Doug
Stahler, Dan
Stebbins, Dan
Sterling, Heather
Sterling, John
Strong, Laura
Stroud, Janice
Temple, Larry
Thurston, Linda
Totten, Charles

Turner, Lisa
Varley, Nathan
Vucetich, John
Vucetich, Lea
Way, Jon
Weigert, Grant
Wengler, Bill
West, Elena
Wilmers, Chris
Wilson, Jason
Wolcott, Michael
Wright, Greg
Wunderlin, Aaron
Yale, Katie
York, Judy
York, Julie
Zieber, Tom

GRAPHS

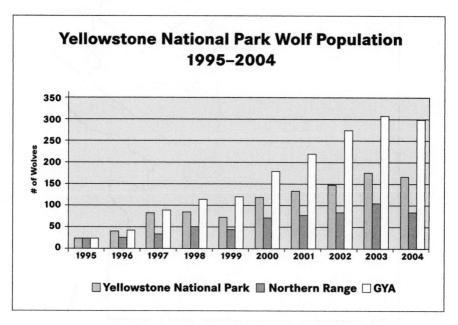

Yellowstone National Park Wolf Population 1995–2004

Wolf population in the Yellowstone area by location from 1995 through 2004. The Northern Range is the portion of Yellowstone with the densest wolf population. The Yellowstone National Park population includes the northern range plus the rest of the park. And finally, GYA (the greater Yellowstone area) represents the park wolf population plus the population of wolves outside the national park. Initially wolf population growth rate was very high, averaging 40 to 50 percent per year for the first five years. It then declined to about 10 percent per year for the next several years, finally stabilizing in 2004.

1995 Yellowstone Wolf Pack Territories

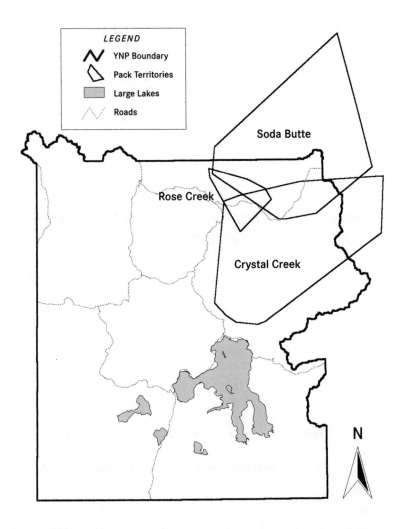

Early on, wolves settled mostly on the northern range. This map shows the wolves' territories in 1995.

2004 Yellowstone Wolf Pack Territories

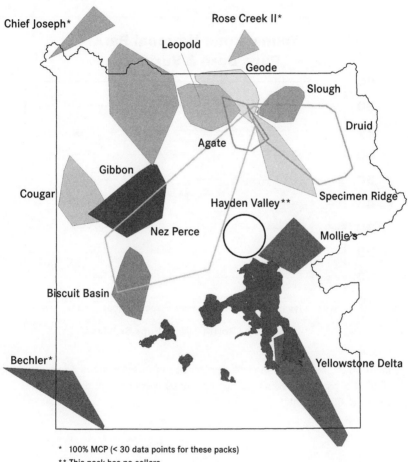

Chief Joseph*

Rose Creek II*

Leopold

Geode

Slough

Druid

Agate

Gibbon

Cougar

Specimen Ridge

Hayden Valley**

Nez Perce

Mollie's

Biscuit Basin

Bechler*

Yellowstone Delta

* 100% MCP (< 30 data points for these packs)
** This pack has no collars

By 2004 the wolves had expanded into areas throughout the park. Yet even today the densest wolf population is located in the northern part of the park, as evidenced here by the greater overlap of territories.

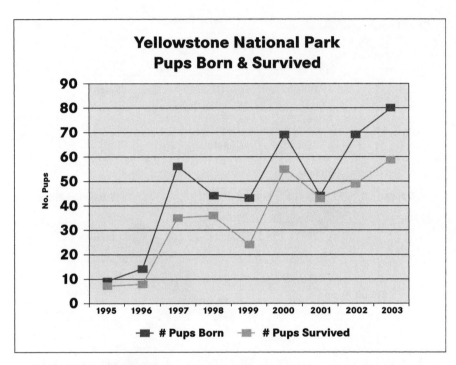

A key factor in the success of the wolf reintroduction to Yellowstone was the production of pups. Most years (1999 being a notable exception), pup survival averaged 75 to 80 percent.

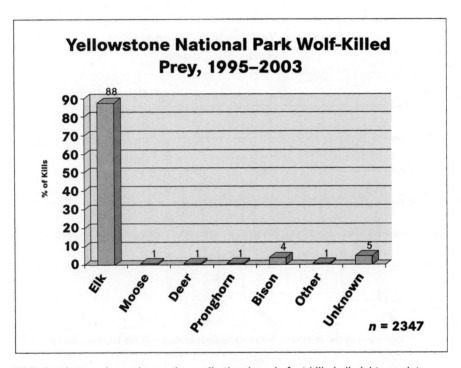

Yellowstone National Park Wolf-Killed Prey, 1995–2003

n = 2347

While in winter wolves rely mostly on elk, they have in fact killed all eight ungulate species living in the park. Deer predation increases in the warm months due to migration of that animal into the park during early summer.

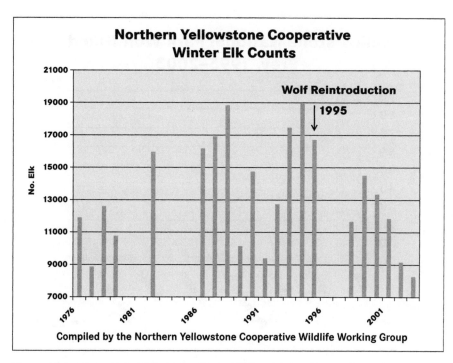

Northern Yellowstone Cooperative Winter Elk Counts

Compiled by the Northern Yellowstone Cooperative Wildlife Working Group

Since wolves were reintroduced into the national park, the elk population has declined by roughly 50 percent. While many attribute this drop entirely to wolves, in fact the elk population was declining before wolves were reintroduced. Elk decline is related to a number of factors, including hunting, drought, and multiple carnivores in addition to wolves.

ENDNOTES

Chapter 1

1. Nowak, R. M. 1995. Another look at wolf taxonomy, pp. 375–397 in L. N. Carbyn, S. H. Fritts, and D. R. Seip, editors, *Ecology and conservation of wolves in a changing world.* Canadian Circumpolar Institute, Edmonton, Alberta.
2. Leonard, J. A., C. Vila, and R. K. Wayne. 2005. Legacy lost: Genetic variability and population size in extirpated US gray wolves. *Molecular Ecology.*
3. Young, S. P. and E. A. Goldman, 1994. *The wolves of North America.* American Wildlife Institute, Washington, D.C.
4. Mech, L. D. 1970. *The wolf: The ecology and behavior of an endangered species.* Natural History Press, Garden City, New York.
5. Jim Hammill quote used with permission, October 2004.
6. Leopold, A. 1949. *A Sand county almanac: With essays on conservation from Round River.* Sierra Club/Ballantine Books, New York.
7. L. D. Mech personal communication, U.S. Geological Survey.
8. Quoted from "The Long Rangers," *Nature Conservancy Magazine,* Fall 2003, quote by Jack Turnell.

Chapter 2
1. Weaver, J. L. 1978. The wolves of Yellowstone. *Natural Resources Report no. 14.* U.S. National Park Service, Washington, D.C. 38pp.
2. J. Leonard, R. Wayne personal communication, UCLA.
3. See chapter 1, Nowak 1995.
4. McNay, M. E. 2002. Wolf-human interactions in Alaska & Canada: A review of the case history. *Wildlife Society Bulletin 30*: 831–843.

Portrait of a Wolf: Number 9
1. R. McIntyre personal communication, Yellowstone National Park.

Chapter 3
1. Fritts, S. H., W. J. Paul and L. D. Mech. 1979. Evaluation of methods for all alleviating wolf depredations on livestock. Unpublished report, USFWS, St. Paul, MN.
2. Taper, M. L. and P. Gogan. 2002. The northern Yellowstone elk: density dependence and climatic conditions. *Journal of Wildlife Management 66*: 106–122.
3. Coppinger, R. and L. Coppinger. 2001. *Dogs: A startling new understanding of canine origin, behavior and evolution.* Scribner, New York.

Chapter 4
1. Varley, J. and W. Brewster. 1992. Wolves for Yellowstone? *Vol. 3. National Park Service Report.*
2. Ibid.
3. Bergman, E. 2003. Assessment of prey vulnerability through analysis of wolf movements and kill sites. Masters Thesis, Montana State University, Bozeman, MT.
4. Messier, F. 1995. On the functional and numerical responses of wolves to changing prey density. In: L. Carbyn, S. Fritts, and D. Seip, editors, pp. 187–197. *Ecology and conservation of wolves in a changing world.* Canadian Circumpolar Institute, Edmonton, Alberta; Eberhardt, L. L. 1997. Is wolf predation ratio-dependant? *Canadian Journal of Zoology 75*: 1940–1944.
5. Observation by R. McIntyre.

6. Peterson, R. 1995. *The wolves of Isle Royale: A broken balance.* Willow
   Creek Press, Minocque, WI. 190pp;
   Mech, L. D. and L. Boitani. 2003. Wolf social ecology. In: L. D.
   Mech and L. Boitani, editors, pp. 1–34, *Wolves: Behavior, ecology and
   conservation.* University of Chicago Press, Chicago and London.
7. Murie, A. 1944. *The wolves of Mount McKinley.* U.S. National Park
   Service Fauna Series, no. 5. U.S. Government Printing Office,
   Washington, D.C. 238pp;
   Pimlott, D. H. 1970. Predation and productivity of game populations
   in North America. *Transactions of International Congress of Game
   Biologists 9*: 63–73.
8. Fuller, T., L. D. Mech and L. F. Cochrane. 2003. Wolf population
   dynamics. In: Mech, L. D. and L. Boitani, editors, pp. 161–191,
   Wolves: Behavior, ecology and conservation. University of Chicago
   Press, Chicago and London.

Portrait of a Wolf: Number 42
1. Observation by R. McIntyre.
2. McIntyre, R. and D. Smith. 2000. The death of a queen: Yellowstone
   mutiny ends tyrannical rule over Druid Pack. *International Wolf*
   10(4):8–11.

Chapter 5
1. Although there is no actual analysis of the type of packs in North
   America, a discussion relating to this issue is available in Dave Mech
   and L. Boitani edited book *Wolves.* See page 164–165 under "Pack
   Composition."
2. Multiple litters have been recorded in other locations and probably
   are more common than once thought since intensive monitoring of
   denning wolves is a recent phenomenon.
3. R. McIntyre personal communication.
4. R. McIntyre personal communication.
5. Mech, L. D., L. F. Adams, T. J. Meier, J. W. Burch and B. W. Dale.
   1998. *The wolves of Denali.* University of Minnesota Press,
   Minneapolis;

Dean Cluff, personal communication, carnivore biologist, Yellowknife, Northwest Territories.

6. Highest ever prey biomass, see discussions in Mech and Boitani, Table 6.2 pp. 167–170; also Fuller, T. K. 1989. Population dynamics of wolves in north-central Minnesota. *Wildlife Monographs*, no. 105. The Wildlife Society.

Chapter 6

1. Wolves for Yellowstone. 1992. A report to the United States Congress. J. Varley and W. Brewster, editors.

2. John Duffield personal communication, University of Montana.

3. McNay, M. E. 2002. Wolf-human interactions in Alaska and Canada: A review of the case history. *Wildlife Society Bulletin 30*: 831–843.

Portrait of a Wolf: Number 14

1. Julie Mao personal communication, University of Alberta.

Chapter 7

1. Berger, J., P. Stacey, L. Bellis, and M. Johnson. 2001. A mammalian predator-prey imbalance: grizzly bear and wolf extinctions affect avian neotropical migrants. *Ecological Applications 11*: 947–960; Nietvelt, C. 2001. Herbivory interactions between beaver (Castor canadensis) and elk (Cervus elaphus) on willow (Salix Spp.) in Banff National Park. Masters Thesis, University of Alberta.

2. Dan Tyers personal communication, Gallatin National Forest.

3. Beschta, R. L. 2003. Cottonwood, elk and wolves in the Lamar valley of Yellowstone National Park. *Ecological Applications 13*: 1295–1309; Ripple, W. J., E. Larsen, R. Renkin, D. Smith. 2001. Trophic cascades among wolves, elk, and aspen on Yellowstone National Parks northern range. *Biological Conservation 102*: 227–234.

4. Wilmers, C., R. Crabtree, D. Smith, K. Murphy, and W. Getz. 2003. Trophic facilitation by introduced top predators: grey wolf subsidies to scavengers in Yellowstone National Park. *Journal of Animal Ecology 72*: 909–916.

5. Stahler, D. R. 2000. Interspecific interactions between the common raven (Corvus corax) and the gray wolf (Canis lupus) in Yellowstone National Park, Wyoming: Investigations of a predator and scavenger relationship. Masters Thesis, University of Vermont, Burlington, VT. 105pp.

6. Crabtree, R. L. and J. W. Sheldon. 1999. The ecological role of coyotes on Yellowstone's Northern Range. *Yellowstone Science 7*: 15–23.

7. Wilmers, C., D. Stahler, R. Crabtree, D. Smith, and W. Getz. 2003. Resource dispersion and consumer dominance: scavenging at wolf- and hunter-killed carcasses in greater Yellowstone, USA. *Ecology Letters 6*: 996–1003.

8. Murphy, K. M. 1998. The ecology of the cougar (Puma concolor) in the northern Yellowstone ecosystem: Interaction with prey, bears, and humans. PhD Dissertation, University of Idaho, Moscow. 147pp.

9. Vucetich, J., R. Peterson, and T. Waite. 2004. Raven scavenging favours group foraging in wolves. *Animal Behaviour*, in press.

10. C. Wilmers personal communication.

11. D. Stahler personal communication.

12. Towne, E. G. 2000. Prairie vegetation and soil nutrient responses to ungulate carcasses. *Oecologia 122*: 232–239.

13. P. J. White personal communication, Yellowstone National Park.

14. See Taper and Gogan, chapter 3.

15. Cook, J. G., B. K. Johnson, R. C. Cook, R. A. Riggs, T. Del Curto, L. D. Bryont, and L. L. Irwin. 2004. Effects of summer-autumn nutrition and parturitiun date on reproduction and survival of elk. *Wildlife Monographs* 155.

16. P. J. White, R. Garrott, L. Eberhardt. 2003. Evaluating the consequences of wolf recovery on Northern Yellowstone elk. *National Park Service Report*, YCR-NR-2004-02.

Chapter 8

1. See Mech and Boitani, chapter 5 and 12 for more details.

2. Dale, B. W., L. G. Adams and R. T. Bowyer. 1994. Functional response of wolves preying on barren-ground caribou in a multi-prey ecosystem. *Journal of Animal Ecology 63*: 644–652.

3. J. Vucetich personal communication.
4. See Wolves for Yellowstone, chapter 6.
5. R. Peterson personal communication.
6. Peterson, R. O. and P. Ciucci. 2003, *The wolf as a carnivore*, see chapter 4 of Mech and Boitani.
7. MacNulty, D. 2002. The predatory sequence and the influence of injury risk on hunting behavior in the wolf. Master's Thesis. University of Minnesota, St. Paul, 71pp.
8. Mech, L. D. 1970. *The wolf: The ecology and behavior of an endangered species*. Natural History Press, Garden City, New York.
9. D. Cluff personal communication, Yellowknife, Northwest Territories.
10. Hall, A. 2003. *Discovering Eden: A lifetime of paddling arctic rivers*. Key Porter Books, Toronto, Canada.
11. P. Frame personal communication.
12. Craighead, J. J., J. S. Sumner, and J. A. Mitchell. 1995. *The grizzly bears of Yellowstone: Their ecology in the Yellowstone ecosystem, 1959–1992*. Island Press, Washington, D.C. 535pp.
13. Mech, L. D., V. B. Kuechte, D. W. Warner, and J. R. Tester. 1965. A collar for attaching radio transmitters to rabbits, hares, and raccoons. *Journal of Wildlife Management* 29: 898–902.
14. R. Peterson personal communication.

Chapter 9

1. C. Gates personal communication.
2. Oakleaf, J., C. Mack, and D. Murray. 2003. Effects of wolves on livestock calf survival and movements in central Idaho. *Journal of Wildlife Management* 67: 299–306.
3. P. J. White personal communication.
4. Ibid.

ABOUT THE AUTHORS

Yellowstone Wolf Project Leader DOUGLAS W. SMITH has studied wolves for twenty-five years. He was a biologist for the world-renowned Isle Royale wolf-moose study, the longest running carnivore study in the world, and has been with the Yellowstone wolf reintroduction since the time of its inception. He is the author of twenty-six scientific publications, nineteen popular articles, thirteen technical reports, six book chapters, and two popular books.

In addition to being an adjunct professor at Montana State University, Doug is a member of the Wildlife Society, American Society of Mammalogists, and the Society for Conservation Biology. When not studying wolves he is a passionate backcountry traveler, most often roaming by canoe the remote rivers of northern Canada.

GARY FERGUSON has been a full-time freelance writer for twenty-two years. He's written for numerous national magazines, including *Vanity Fair, Outside,* and *Men's Journal,* and is the author of fourteen books on nature and science. Ferguson's recent title, *Hawks Rest: A Season in the Remote Heart of Yellowstone* (2003, National Geographic), was chosen a nonfiction book of the year by both the Pacific Northwest and the Mountains and Plains bookseller's associations. Gary and his wife, Jane, live at the edge of the greater Yellowstone ecosystem. For more information about Gary and his books, log on to www.wildwords.net.

INDEX

Weaver, John, 29
Whales, 24
Whitebark pine, 124
Whitelaw, Alice, 23
White-tailed deer, 145, 183
Whooping cranes, 24
Wilderness
  impact of wolves, 14–16, 117–31
  protected, 8, 14
Wildlife. *See also* specific animals
  in Lamar Valley, 46
  and television, 107–8
Williams, Pat, 99
Willow recovery, 119–21
Winter
  of 1996–97, 129–30
  movement in, 148
Winter Study, 139, 140–41
Wolf Wars (Fischer), 26
Wolves. *See also* specific packs
  and acclimation pens, 47–51, 57
  alpha pair, 88, 89–90, 92
  behavior of, 15–16, 91–92, 104–6, 137–38
  breeding, 88–91
  capturing/radio collaring, 148–66
  changes in population, 85–86, 169–71
  den study, 146–47
  early research on, 107
  feelings about, 8, 9–10, 30–33, 98–101, 107–8
  homing response of, 47–48
  impact on ecosystem, 14–16, 118–31
  and livestock, 46, 172–75
  monitoring kills, 65, 138–46
  in North America, 7–8, 14, 87, 183–85
  packs of, 23, 71–72, 86–87, 121–22
  reintroduction of, 10–11, 14, 25–30, 32–33

status of packs, 175–82
subspecies of, 29–30
territorial instinct of, 64–67, 71–72, 75–76
Wood Buffalo National Park, 14, 90
Wyoming
  managing wolves, 171
  reducing elk herds, 33

Y

Yale, Katie, 164
Yellowstone National Park. *See also* Yellowstone Wolf Project
  changes in population, 87–92, 169–71
  elk herd in, 45–47, 64, 119, 127–31, 176
  northern and interior packs, 64–65, 175–82
  weather/climate in, 128–29, 130
  wolf poaching in, 9
  wolf watching in, 97–100, 101–3, 106–8
  wolves and ecosystem, 14–16, 15–16, 118–31
Yellowstone Wolf Project
  acclimations pens, 23, 47–51, 57
  den study, 146–47
  and radio collaring, 148–66
  reintroduction of wolves, 10–11, 14, 25–30, 32–33
  reintroduction team, 181–82
  and Sawtooth pups, 56
  success of, 182–83
  trapping in Canada, 19–24
  Winter Study, 139–46
  worldwide interest in, 11
Yukon, 14